The eight papers in this volume were initially presented at a
conference entitled 'The Future of the Rural Landscape in Ireland'
held at Trinity College, Dublin in March, 1985. There has been
only slight revision of their original form. Organised by the
Department of Geography in Trinity in conjunction with the Irish
Planning Institute, the conference had as its chief aim to initiate
informed discussion about the future form and appearance of
Ireland's rural landscape, a topic hitherto relatively neglected.
Among the 80 participants were representatives of a wide range of
interested institutions and professional bodies in the Republic
and Northern Ireland. It was the purpose of the papers to examine
the impact of man's present and future activities on the appearance
and visual quality of rural areas, to emphasise new landscape
elements and note features of aesthetic, historical, recreational,
or wild life importance which might soon be lost. Attention was
expressly devoted not merely to areas of outstanding scenic quality
but to the rural landscape as a whole and it was decided that the
necessary breadth of perspective could best be achieved by focuss-
ing on patterns of change within basic components of the landscape
i.e. settlements, the farmed countryside, forests, and bogs. Concern for the landscape was combined with practical proposals for
its good management and the papers suggest a wide range of action
to help conserve and, if possible, enhance landscape quality.

i

Although of considerable beauty and interest the Irish landscape
is not treated with sufficient care or respect and has frequently
been abused by private and public activities. If, as seems likely,
the character of the countryside is now in the early stages of
rapid and far-reaching transformation then carefully considered
and co-ordinated action will be necessary on many fronts to ensure
that landscape quality is preserved. As far as possible, future
landscape policies should represent the whole community and not
only the small minority of farmers and landowners who presently
control the shaping of the landscape. There is a clear, inescapable
need to build better relationships and understanding between
farming, forestry, recreational activities, and countryside and
nature conservation. This is an important reason for making these
papers available in book form to a wide audience. There is no
unanimity of outlook among the writers but they represent a variety
of professional viewpoints (human geography, folk life, landscape
architecture, ecology and planning) and their contributions should
certainly help to stimulate and inform wide-ranging debate.

Contributions to the cost of preparing and printing the papers have
been made by the following :

>   The Provost's Development Fund, Trinity College,
>   Bord na Mona,
>   Bord Failte.

Without the support of these bodies production of the papers would
not have been possible and I am grateful to them for their interest
and generous assistance.

The following acted as chairmen at the various sessions during the
conference and contributed to the generally high quality of dis-
cussion : Mr. P. O hUigin, Secretary, Dept. of the Taoiseach;
Professor J.A. Fehily, Dept. of Regional and Urban Planning,
University College, Dublin; Mr. R. Stringer, Dept. of Environment;
Miss J. Caffrey, President, Irish Planning Institute.

Finally, among the many who assisted with the conference, I am
specially indebted to Mr. C. Lynch, Executive Planning Officer,
Laois Co. Council, for sustained advice and assistance; to Dr. J.
Fehan for arranging, at short notice, an excellent exhibition of
photographs and maps illustrating the landscape survey presently
being carried out by the Roscrea Heritage Society, and to Mrs. E.
Russell, Secretary, Dept. of Geography, Trinity College, for help
with the organisation of the conference and the typing of the
papers.

F.H.A. Aalen
Dept. of Geography
Trinity College Dublin

CONTENTS

iv

THE RURAL LANDSCAPE : CHANGE, CONSERVATION AND PLANNING

F.H.A. Aalen

Owing to a variety of economic and social forces the rural landscapes in many European countries have been rapidly transformed in
recent decades, sometimes with a marked reduction of their scenic,
historic and wildlife appeal. Concern has been widespread (Crowe,
1964, Fairbrother, 1972: Countryside Commission, 1977: Millman and
Brandon, 1978, 1980, 1981). Aware of the risks of misguided development, some countries, for example West Germany and Holland, have
taken legal, organisational, and financial measures to protect their
rural landscape and plan its development (Niggemann, von Kurten,
1980; Schuyf, 1978).

In Ireland there has been no abrupt, wholesale change of the
countryside. Changes have been, in the main, incremental but in total
they are appreciable and some may constitute the early stages of major
transformations. Landscape conservation and planning, unlike rural
economic and social problems, have generated little discussion, concern or study and few practical initiatives; something which this
collection of papers aims to correct. The main objectives here are
to examine, first, the impact of man's present and future activities
on the lay-out and appearance of rural areas, and, second, the steps
which might be taken to conserve and, if possible, enhance landscape
quality, defined as the ability of the landscape to satisfy the
aesthetic, intellectual and recreational demands of society. Emphasis
is placed on the role of the planner, but the problems clearly require
a many-sided, co-ordinated approach. It is sometimes argued that

I

nothing effective can be accomplished in the sphere of landscape conservation and planning since landscape quality is purely a matter of individual taste. However, there is appreciable agreement on basics and considerable progress could be made without being diverted into questions of personal preferences (Shine, this volume). Research into landscape evaluation and preferences may eventually help to establish objective visual criteria but work is still in a pioneer stage and rarely very helpful to planners (Newby, 1979).

The rural landscape is a synthesis of natural and man-made features, evolved over many thousands of years, including terrain, vegetation cover, settlement and field patterns, and routeways (Mitchell, 1976; Aalen, 1978). It is the setting, indeed partly the artefact, of farming and forestry, and a habitat for wildlife, but also an immense aesthetic, cultural and historical legacy, both expressing and shaping national and regional identity. Perhaps it is no exaggeration to claim the rural landscape as a major national artistic achievement and it is the pleasure derived from simply view-ing the landscape which attracts most people to the countryside. It is well established too that our rural landscape is a substantial economic asset because of its attraction to tourists, and the land-scape provides the setting for and its beauty enhances the enjoyment of a wide range of recreational, sporting and educational activities (Mawhinney, 1979; Buchanan, 1982). The quality of the landscape, not merely at the most scenic spots but as a whole, must be a major national concern.

Discussion of landscape change cannot be divorced from changing patterns of economic land use and the growth and redistribution of

population and settlement. The growing efficiency and changed
methods of farming, encouraged by state finance, considerably
influence the landscape, modifying the field patterns through
enclosure removal and expanding the farmed area at the expense of
natural and semi-natural habitats by reclamation and drainage
projects. New obtrusive farm buildings are a further facet of
change. Afforestation and commercial exploitation of peat bogs
have also had considerable impact, as well as recreational and
tourism growths. Planning has had little influence on these developments, since most are exempted from planning controls. Economic and
population growth since the 1960's and a weak planning structure
have encouraged a profusion of single houses in the countryside, one
of the most striking aspects of visual change. Later papers in this
volume will develop these major topics and make specific proposals
as to how landscape quality could be safeguarded and improved. The
writers are all professionally involved with the landscape or elements
in it and their views, while not necessarily in agreement, must serve
to stimulate and inform discussion of landscape policies. Numerous
issues with an important bearing on the rural landscape are not considered here and must await treatment at some later date. They
include industrial infrastructure in the rural areas, such as power
lines and new roads with the sometimes unsightly paraphernalia along
them, and also quarrying and mining, still sometimes uninfluenced by
modern techniques of screening and landscape restoration. Omitted
too is the widespread problem of litter and unsightly concentrations
of rubbish and dereliction in the countryside.

THE FARMED LANDSCAPE

Drainage and Reclamation

Because of agriculture's important position in the Irish economy farmers in recent decades have been successfully encouraged by their advisers and educators and by government grants to expand agricultural production. More efficient farming however has rarely been tempered by wider considerations, such as the visual effects of innovations. The practices having the greatest landscape impact are drainage and reclamation of land, removal of hedgerows and other field boundaries, new houses and the construction of large farm buildings.

In a countryside with an excess of moisture, drainage projects are key elements in reclamation. They underlay some of the most impressive landlord improvements carried out in the 18th and 19th centuries and have received state encouragement since the time of the Congested Districts Board. The extensive arterial and field drainage schemes of the present day are largely financed by state capital, boosted since 1978 by EEC grants. Arterial drainage has affected mainly the lowland river basins, while drainage, heavy machinery and artificial fertilizers have permitted reclamation and improvement of rough upland environments. Whatever the economic justification for the drainage and reclamation schemes may be, there have clearly been environmental losses, to fishing and wild life for example, and to aesthetic qualities through the unsightly spoil heaps along the deepened channels. Among the many features removed from the landscape are remnants of historic settlement, sometimes scarcely identifiable by the farmers. Inevitably, schemes of agricultural modernisation will entail some loss of historical heritage but the

4

remarkable richness of the Irish countryside in this respect needs special emphasis (Reeves-Smith and Hamond, 1983). Reclamation and improvement projects must consequently proceed with special caution and responsibility. We do not have adequate information to calculate the nature and quantity of recent destruction over the landscape as a whole but local investigations show clearly that it has been substantial (Fehan 1979, Barry 1979, R.S.A.I., 1983).

Fields

Fields, enclosed by hedgerows, banks and walls, are the essence of the Irish rural landscape, distinguishing it from many other parts of Europe, but average field size is below the optimum for modern farm machinery and on small farms the removal of banks can significantly increase the area of productive land. Steady enlargement of fields and general rationalisation of farm layout, with a widening and straightening of access roads and lanes for example, are underway on many farms. No study of the extent of these processes has been undertaken and it is hard to assess how far they will go. Ireland may be in the early stages of the far-reaching processes of change experienced in a number of European countries, but thorough-going transformation has usually been associated with progressive arable farming and the pastoral bent of Irish farming could be some restraint. Any widespread removal of field enclosures in Ireland should be carefully assessed on economic and ecological grounds and would certainly seriously erode the attractiveness and diversity of the landscape. However, the present partial removal of hedges and banks is unlikely to be very harmful. Many of them originated within the last two centuries or so and are floristically poor. Neither is their removal always visually detrimental. Irish hedgerows are often

5

Fig. 1. Near Mitchelstown, co. Cork. The landscape here owes much of its character to the rectangular hedged fields. New forest on the hillsides is a further striking element.

Fig. 2. Above Blessington lake, co. Wicklow. Dry-stone walling around irregular field shapes is the dominant feature of the countryside. Traditional buildings are low and unobtrusive. The contrast between the enclosed fields and the unimproved higher land is a striking feature.

overgrown and unsightly and shut out vistas, especially along roadsides. In places with low undulating relief their removal could
reveal the subtler landforms and might enhance the landscape.

The historical significance of fields and field shapes, however,
is little appreciated or understood. Although the greater part of
the present-day field pattern originated during the 17th, 18th and
19th centuries, some fields reflect the agrarian organisation of
much earlier periods and are a significant historical legacy. For
example, the long, narrow slightly curved fields sometimes found
around pale villages are a relic of medieval, open-field strip systems.
Unfortunately, some of the best examples, including those at Rathcoole
and Newcastle in co. Dublin, have already been destroyed by modern
housing developments. Small irregular fields, often found on old
commons and in hill areas, may reflect the high population pressure
and squatting of smallholders in pre-Famine times. In some hill areas
the field boundaries may even have survived from remote prehistoric
times, and conspicuous enclosures often mark the limits of ancient
townlands or estates. On historical grounds then, complete preservation of the field pattern in some localities may be desirable, but
these clearly can be of only limited extent. Generally we must
accept that field patterns will undergo modification in the interests
of farm efficiency. Wholesale, careless eradication, however, should
be discouraged. Even in schemes of radical reorganisation it is
usually possible to retain certain significant field boundaries of
historic, wild life or aesthetic value without impediment to the work
of farmers, or perhaps to retain the main part of hedgerows but with
broad openings in them through which heavy machinery can easily pass.
The work of the Countryside Commission in Britain under its New

Agricultural Landscapes programme shows how, with the aid of willing
farmers, good farming and conservation of cultural landscape
features and wild life can sometimes be reconciled, providing there
is a plan for the future development of the farm, taking into account
multiple objectives.

Rural buildings

Rural buildings can give the countryside an unmistakable stamp.
In Ireland the numerous dispersed farmsteads are a particularly
important scenic element but over the last two or three decades
buildings with any traditional or regional character have rapidly
declined in number, much to the detriment of the landscape. The
tendency everywhere has been to build in urban styles and any rural
distinctiveness and regional differences have been almost lost.
This may in part reflect some deep rejection of all connections with
an impoverished peasant past but even in the richer rural areas where
there was a tradition of substantial vernacular buildings (in
Wexford, Tipperary and Louth, for example) there is little or no
evidence of concern to adapt and preserve them or to develop new
forms even remotely in sympathy with the old. Country people seem
unaware of the interest and attractiveness of traditional buildings
and of any alternative to the unimaginative urban models now used in
the countryside.

Some progress has been made with the conservation and preservation of rural houses in Northern Ireland (Gailey, 1984 and this volume).
There is, however, no adequate legal and financial provision for
comparable work in the Republic and architects have shown virtually
no interest in rural building traditions or the development of
regional styles. It is difficult now to see how any feeling of

7

regional coherence or tradition can be re-established in rural
building. Something of great value has been lost and while the new
wave of housing may be a considerable advance socially it rarely
enhances the landscape.

The situation is similar with farm buildings. Compared with
many European countries the barns and other outbuildings on Irish
farms are architecturally unimpressive but the compact grouping of
elementary functional structures can be aesthetically satisfying.
Many buildings, however, are now quite obsolete and have either been
destroyed or, more often, left to decay. Some old farm buildings,
but only a fraction, might in the future serve to accommodate small-
scale manufacturing or service enterprises in the countryside of the
kind which planning authorities in Britain and elsewhere are now
actively encouraging as valuable sources of employment for the rural
community. But most old buildings will fall into unsightly dereliction. There is a general demand for larger, cheap, versatile
buildings whose materials, colour and texture may be alien to the
local landscape. With careful attention to detail, design and colour,
and to siting and the surroundings, it is possible to harmonise the
new with the old and even make a positive contribution to the landscape. Much can be achieved through specialist advice, but it is
difficult to find evidence of this in the Irish countryside. Clutter
and rubbish in and around farmyards and rural settlements is often
conspicuous, even spectacular, and a general clearing-up would considerably improve the rural areas. How this could ever be induced
is hard to envisage.

Rural suburbanisation

Change within agriculture is not the only influence on rural building. During the last 25 years, as economic life noticeably quickened, there was a reversal of the long-standing trend of congestion and population decline. With the major exception of tourism, new economic activity and employment is industrial and usually urban-based but it has had repercussions in the countryside. With growing affluence and mobility many urban workers and retired people increasingly settle in rural areas. Small towns and villages along major arteries leading to Dublin and other regional centres have grown markedly, but conspicuous too are the lines of new houses (the favoured form is the bungalow) lining the roads in the open countryside within commuting distance of town and city (Duffy, 1983). Some areas of high scenic quality relatively remote from major urban centres, such as the shores of Lough Derg and coastal Donegal, have also attracted roadside concentrations of retirment and summer houses. Rural suburbanisation (see Shaffrey this volume) raises numerous problems, among them sewage and effluent problems, traffic hazards, and strong visual and aesthetic impacts. Bungalows are often ostentatious in design, prominently sited and at odds with the rural surroundings, while trees and hedges are removed from the roadsides and replaced by brick walls.

House building in rural areas is subject to planning control, and the diffuse pattern of rural settlement contrary to the stated policies of central and local government. Numerous authorities make explicit reference to the undesirability of scattered rural housing but there is a serious failure in the implementation of policies.

FORESTS

Forests, public and private, occupy about 5 per cent of the Republic's land surface. Private forests are beginning to grow but the private sector is conspicuously small by European standards. The private woods are predominantly deciduous, scattered in small areas in the lowlands and frequently associated with the old demesnes. Although small in area they are of importance scenically and for wild life. Unfortunately many have been neglected and require care and conservation. The bulk of the country's forests (about 85 per cent) is recent state afforestation, 95 per cent of it coniferous, concentrated on low quality but scenic land especially on the middle slopes of mountain areas. State policy has been to avoid afforestation on good land. In recent years over half of new planting has been on bogland, an important trend likely to continue and to influence deeply the landscape of lowlands and uplands. The possibilities have recently been discussed of afforestation of the drumlin belt, where soils available to the uneconomic small farms are poorly suited to agriculture yet ideal for forests. Private afforestation has commenced there but seems unlikely to produce extensive and continuous forests in the near future. Integration of these small woods into the drumlin landscape poses interesting new challenges for landscape design.

Apart from their economic importance state forests have numerous merits, including provision for recreation and wild life which private forests would be unlikely to make on a comparable scale. Furthermore, forests, if carefully designed and planted, can add to the diversity and attractiveness of the landscape and serve a variety of landscape design purposes. They have, for example, great capacity for absorbing

visitors and recreational facilities and may be the only landscape
elements adequate in scale to reduce the impact of large intrusions
such as roads, pylon lines, quarries and industries. But the
forests should 'fit' the landscape, be in sympathy with and even
enhance natural features. Criticism of forests arises partly from
instinctive dislike of extensive landscape change, but the unsympathetic shape, scale and uniformity of the forests are probably
more significant. Priority has been given to rapid planting of the
maximum area with the most productive species. A policy of consolidation now operates but, until recently, land was acquired
wherever available and geometric forest shapes have resulted from
planting within the boundaries of the purchased properties. Symmetry,
parallel lines, right angles and excessive repetition are unsympathetic to flowing and irregular landforms and should be avoided. The
undifferentiated mass of the forest can disrupt the balance and
diversity of the landscape, submerging it with an unbroken blanket
of trees which, especially in the lowlands, obscures attractive small-
scale scenery. The commencement of large-scale felling will initiate
new problems; then there could be unsightly breaches, unless the
process is sensitively controlled.

Forestry is an activity which in a relatively short time causes
massive changes in the landscape visible for decades and even
centuries. But it should now be possible by careful and sensitive
landscape design to reconcile the beauty of the landscape with the
economic demands placed on it. In 1972 Nan Fairbrother wrote that
much of the bad work of the Forestry Commission in Britain was early
and that recent planting was "re-assuringly landscape conscious".
What would our verdict be on Irish planting? New plantings in west

11

Wicklow, for example, still have geometrical edges and cut the bare granitic domes into unnatural shapes. Kennedy and McCusker (1983) state that, since the mid-1960's, when Irish forests were undergoing rapid expansion, there has been recognition of the need to tailor whole plantations to good landscape principles, so as to marry plantations into the surrounding countryside more successfully. The same authors make reference to the existence of a strong, state, landscape management and recreational policy. They note and regret that little of this policy is available for scrutiny in public documents.

As the extent of the forests grows, their appearance and lay-out will become more contentious and land use conflicts may sharpen. It will be increasingly necessary to decide where landscape change is acceptable and where not and ensure that change is planned in full knowledge of its consequences.

BOGS

Bogs make up approximately one-sixth of the total land area. Both major types, the blanket bogs and the raised bogs, are dominated by natural vegetation but there are differences in their landscapes and land uses (van Eck et al. 1984). The blanket bogs are more extensive, their vast treeless vistas largely dominated by the relatively thin peat layer itself, covering and closely following the underlying topography. Regional contrasts in blanket bog landscapes occur, reflecting the underlying geomorphology. For example, blanket bogs with smooth rolling outlines have developed over the granitic domes of the Leinster mountains while on the surface of the coastal lowlands of Connemara the bogs are level and lake-strewn.

Raised bogs, or lowland bogs, are normally smaller in area and scattered over the central lowlands where they originated in damp hollows in the undulating surface of the glacial drift. Their open character and natural vegetation contrasts with the improved, enclosed and settled landscape on the better-drained surfaces around them.

Patterns of actual and potential land use on the bog types are different, as well as the nature of land-use conflicts. Blanket bogs are widely used for rough grazing and can be reclaimed for grassland. They are, moreover, suited to forests and in recent decades state afforestation has increased strongly on the blanket bogs of the western seaboard and major mountain masses throughout the country. This trend seems likely to continue, diminishing the vastness of these unique landscapes, partially concealing them and introducing geometrical elements into their natural scenery. However, blanket bogs are likely to survive as significant land-scape elements; in general, land use conflicts are less pronounced here than on the raised bogs, and it might be possible therefore to work out sensible long-term land-use and landscape policies.

The virgin raised bogs are less suited to forests, and not suited for agricultural purposes, save on reclaimed areas of cut-away bog. They are, however, more attractive than the blanket bogs for commercial turf production. All the large raised bogs, about one fifth of the total by surface area, have now been acquired for development by Bord na Mona. By early in the next century most may be gone and only the bottom layer left. Future use of these cut-away bogs will indeed be one major determinant of the landscape of many parts of the low-lying centre of Ireland. The lower layer of peat when mixed by deep ploughing with the underlying mineral materials provides soils whose productive potential varies considerably over short distances. Even small areas of cut-away bog can be of a complex nature and unlikely to be suitable for any one use. Certain portions are best suited to grassland, others to forestry, and only small localities to arable. Certain tracts of cut-away bog could be flooded for amenity and recreational purposes, or allowed to revert to natural vegetation attractive to wild life and recreation. The eventual patterns of land use cannot be foreseen, much depending on the pattern of ownership, but it does seem that the strong contrast between the natural bog and the surrounding cultural landscape will disappear. Perhaps some guidelines for the design of the future landscape should be worked out? How extensive should forest be and how laid out? Are the new grazing lands to be enclosed by ditches and hedges as on the surrounding landscapes?

The preservation of a range of totally untouched bogs is urgently required to meet not only scientific, wild life and archaeological interests but landscape consideration too. Since landscapes untouched by man are becoming rare in Europe, Ireland's bogs represent a major scenic resource. Our lowland blanket bogs are unique and raised bogs now confined to Ireland. But only a small part of the total peatland area is of special importance to conservation interests, and concern with it should not lead us to forget that the bulk of the bogs is destined to disappear and to overlook the issue of the future scenic character of the exploited areas.

LANDSCAPE CONSERVATION AND PLANNING

A major objective of this publication is to initiate discussion
of the steps which might be taken to conserve and if possible enhance
landscape quality. Respect for the inherited visual character and
historical identity of regions is desirable but, save in exceptional
circumstances, the landscape cannot be 'frozen' in its current condition. Constant adjustment is needed to meet new economic and
social needs and especially in response to developments in agricultural technology. Is it possible to guide landscape change over the
long-term so that the aesthetic and intellectual appeal of the
landscape is maintained or re-created, with minimum interference to
the efficiency of agriculture, forestry and other rural activities?
Who will decide the guidelines? What will they comprise? How could
they be implemented? The tasks are substantial. It will be
necessary to identify and retain visually, historically, and
ecologically valuable landscape elements, integrating them with the
new. Solid evidence will have to be provided for all decisions
about conservation priorities. Future developments in a wide range
of rural activities must be decisively tempered by concern for landscape quality. Practical procedures must be devised for carrying
all of this out in a comprehensive and co-ordinated way.

At present there is no clear policy on these matters and our
planning system is probably too weak to implement any. Ireland
still lacks any government body specially responsible for rural
conservation interests, nothing comparable to the Countryside
Commission in England and in Scotland for example, and our National
Parks are few and small in area. The Irish countryside, even more
than the British, is at the mercy of the farmers who own and develop

it. Moreover, the information base for policy design and implementation, knowledge of the content of the landscape and current changes
in it, is seriously deficient. Conscious public concern for the
countryside is beginning to grow but is still too weak and un-
organised to influence appreciably the agencies and individuals
responsible for change. Strong, rural-based organisations, comparable
for example to the Farming and Wildlife Advisory Group in England
and Wales or the Society for the Preservation of Rural England,
from which an informed conservation viewpoint could issue, are still
lacking. However, the establishment in 1985 of the Farming and
Conservation Liaison Group by An Taisce is a welcome development on
the Irish scene. This new group aims to improve understanding by
farmers and conservationists of each others viewpoints, to demon-
strate that good farming and the conservation of wildlife and
landscape need not conflict, and to promote ideas and methods of
conservation on the farm. Clearly, many difficult questions require
answering before a satisfactory landscape policy can be formulated
and effectively implemented. Policy will, for example, be more
effective if linked with broader land-use policies. It is not,
however, identical with them. Land-use policies have to be trans-
lated into appropriate landscape. We could achieve the best economic
use of our land resources and preserve our wild life but still
produce a wretched landscape, unless landscape quality becomes a
major consideration in our land-use activities. We need to
remember here that rural land-use planning is slight or non-existent
and our planners, still educated to deal mainly with urban problems,
have limited understanding of the ecological history of regions,
the problems of farming and forestry and of landscape design.

Although an important element of the total conservation
interest, nature conservation has not been made a prominent consideration in this volume. Nature conservation and landscape
quality are overlapping considerations with much in common but
only a small part of the landscape is of special interest to
nature conservation and the concern of this publication is with
the total landscape. Nelson and Brady (1979) have written that
''an adequate conservation programme would probably entail restricting the use of no more than about half of one per cent of the land
area''. However, a much more complete pattern of nature reserves
is needed than at present, large enough to accommodate representative samples of indigenous flora and fauna, with appropriate
organisation and management. A modest start has been made and
crucial legal difficulties overcome by the Wildlife Act, 1976 which
gives power to the Ministry of Fisheries and Forestry to undertake
conservation studies and to acquire and manage nature reserves.
Ireland, however, is still far from any effective nature conservation policy (Lang, 1983).

Certain characteristics of rural landscapes make them more
difficult to protect and administer in the public interest than are
buildings and individual sites. The built environment is in defined
units of known date and well understood function. But rural landscapes are an inextricable fusion of natural and cultural elements
whose age, function and relationship we rarely understand. Regional
varieties of landscape are readily appreciated but it is difficult
to define their boundaries. Moreover, the forces of change and
destruction are often insidious. Changes, especially if they are
incremental, can be thrust upon the landscape before anybody notices

or complains. Seasonal changes and the cyclic activities of man may help to mask deeper permananent alteration. As Shoard (1981) has remarked, the apparent ability to regenerate can create the dangerous illusion that landscapes once savaged can be relied on to heal their own wounds. Perhaps most significant in explaining our lack of concern with the rural landscape, especially in Ireland, is that it appears to be inexhaustible. Even if one tract is marred we are ready to assume that there is plenty more unspoilt over the hill or horizon. So the very extent of our countryside may encourage an uncaring, irresponsible attitude to its protection. Things do not become precious unless their supply is clearly threatened.

Should we aim to inject landscape quality into every major land use or concentrate efforts on selected tracts of highly scenic landscape which would be given special protected status? It is sometimes argued that the ecological conflict in objectives between exploitative agricultural use and protective amenity use for land-scape, wild life and historic conservation is so fundamental that polarisation of land use is inevitable (Green, 1975; Fairbrother, 1970). If areas are to be maintained for conservation purposes then, the argument continues, they must be planned and managed out-side the agricultural/exploitative system: if they are to be viable alongside intensively farmed landscape then the bigger they are the better. The farmed countryside could then be run and transformed solely in the interests of intensive agriculture. It is debatable and perhaps doubtful whether developments in Ireland will necessitate such an approach. Compared with most European countries population pressure and recreational demands on the countryside are still relatively slight. Even in the productive regions of the east and south the numerous scattered hill masses, bogs and ill-drained areas will naturally encourage a varied mosaic pattern of landscape and land-use with an intermingling of unimproved land, of intensive and extensive farming. In the unproductive parts natural features will remain prominent, providing a diverse system of wildlife habitats and a potential network of areas accessible for recreation. Intensive arable farming, which is the most exclusive form of land use, is confined to very limited areas and there are no highly specialised arable zones. The dominant pattern of livestock farming is more congenial to other rural activities. Thus, even in the rich farming areas some compromise between farmers and others may yet be achievable so that modern agricultural practices can function along with wild life, amenity and an interesting and beautiful countryside. Indeed, the presence of a substantial and growing number of urban-orientated residents in the countryside will surely dent the traditional hegemony of the farmers. Compromise will not occur unless actively encouraged and facilitated by official bodies, farming organisations, educational agencies and the media. Unfortunately, farm size and ownership patterns may not be favourable to conservation interests. Almost all Irish farmers are owner-occupiers working holdings of modest size and therefore with every incentive to invest in production improvements but unready or unable to make financial sacrifices in the interest of conservation. In Britain it is striking how often the best-kept landscapes and the most progressive farming are associated with large estates and large farms of a kind absent in this country.

Rural landscape policies with clearly stated and reasonably detailed objectives are required, avoiding vague platitudes and

and abstractions politically acceptable but unhelpful in practice. Effective implementation is also needed and little will be achieved here without energetic and well-targeted educational and advisory programmes. The available techniques of impplementation include voluntary implementation, requiring particularly extensive support from educational and advisory services, financial and other incentives, and planning controls (Countryside Commission, 1974). How far can landscape management rely on self-regulation and voluntary agreements between the various rural interests, with the planner perhaps serving mainly as a mediator or advisor? There are obvious advantages if objectives can be achieved without the use of imposed powers. Codes of Practice (such as recommended for foresters by Dunstan in this volume) might be useful, especially if worked out with local planning authorities and made public, although it is hard to see how their application could be monitored and guaranteed without some degree of public control. Landscape conservation could be facilitated by financial and other inducements, especially in the extensive areas of impecunious small farms. In general where grant-aided improvements are concerned there is much to be said for arrangements in which producers are provided with co-ordinated advice on their proposed schemes with environmental and aesthetic considerations taken fully into account from the start. This seems to call for some cooperation between local planning authorities and institutions responsible for the provision of grants. Comprehensive care of the landscape could not be achieved in this way, however, since some farm 'modernisation' is undertaken without the help of grants.

Fig. 3

a) Deserted demesne, Ballinatray house, co. Waterford. Many fine landscapes of this sort urgently require care and imaginative use.

b) Inistioge, co. Kilkenny. It is vital with such small village-like settlements to retain their architectural character and coherence and a clear demarcation with the countryside. (Bord Fáilte).

If voluntary approaches fail should there be resort to an extension of planning controls to the countryside, with farming and forestry made publicly accountable in advance for any changes they wish to make? Is this feasible, given the predictable resistance of the farmers and other users of rural resources, the limited public and political support for planning and dissatisfaction with its performance in urban areas? These questions have been widely debated in Britain and are still answered there in the negative. Of course, whether agreements or controls are used, there will have to be clear design guidelines. Controls imply reasonably detailed objectives for the overall structure of the landscape, while agreements would have to be compatible with them and linked into a large-scale whole.

Eventually some feasible combination of advice, incentives and controls may be worked out, suited to Irish conditions and adjustable to regional needs. Special measures will, for example, be required on the fringes of cities and towns and in highly scenic areas. To obtain high quality landscapes the approach must be comprehensive and activities co-ordinated. Could all this be carried out by reform of the imperfect planning institutions we already have or will new institutions and mechanisms be needed? Should direction and control come from the centre rather than rely on local government which has so singularly failed in the one sphere of rural development over which it has control, namely housing (Shaffrey, this volume).

Detailed proposals on the formulation and implementation of landscape policies are perhaps premature. What is important now is official recognition of basic problems. The Department of Environment might be best suited to initiate new thinking and approaches, although effective policies will require agreement and co-ordinated action on many fronts, and various ministries require conversion to environmentally sympathetic policies.

Much fuller knowledge and appreciation of the character and content of our landscapes and their regional variation is required as a basis for landscape protection and enhancement schemes, for effective monitoring of landscape change, and in order to heighten public awareness of the beauty, interest and intricacy of the countryside. Scholarly, affectionate interpretation of our landscape is much needed, suitably presented for the reading public. Professional geographers, with a few outstanding exceptions, have so far failed in this important task.

Other than the incomplete and seriously outdated, large-scale Ordnance Survey maps we have no detailed record of our landscape. Aerial photographs are a useful supporting source of information but ultimately there is no substitute for detailed, painstaking survey on the ground with careful recording and classification. Using the O.S. sheets as a basis it should be possible to compile accurate inventories of the total assemblage of features making up the ordinary landscape including for example enclosure and walling methods, gate posts, house types, field patterns and road systems, and not simply outstanding historic or archaeological sites. In recent years some progress has been made in this kind of comprehensive landscape mapping, in Holland, Germany, and parts of England for example (Millman and Brandon, 1978, 1980). Local historical, amenity and heritage groups can play an important part in the work, but their efforts should be co-ordinated and some standardised approach adopted in different parts of the country.

Their projects could then be integrated into strategic landscape plans for each county. Useful pioneer work has now been carried out by Roscrea Heritage Society in conjunction with AnCO, which could serve as a model and inspiration for projects elsewhere. Such surveys can have important educational effects. They can be used to familiarise those in schools, the general public and, not least, farmers, with the range and significance of landscape components. Farmers intending to carry out 'improvements' should be able to obtain local advice on the scenic and historic value of the patches they control, and encouraged to do so.

The countryside also requires closer study to identify any important spatial variations in the pace and character of landscape change. Different approaches may be required in the various areas and priority given to those of high scenic value experiencing rapid change. Sample areas, with differing geology, soils and farming types, should be investigated with, in each area, consideration of how economic changes, especially agricultural improvements and forestry, can be carried out efficiently with minimum reduction of the visual, historical and other qualities of the landscape. Capacity to anticipate landscape changes would be strengthened by deeper understanding of the economic and social forces influencing the use of our varied rural resources. These are high priorities in any country concerned with the future of its landscapes.

References

Aalen, F.H.A., Man and the Landscape in Ireland, London, 1978.

An Foras Forbartha, Inventory of Outstanding Landscapes in Ireland, 1977.

Barry, T.B., 'The Destruction of Irish Archaeological Monuments' in Irish Geography, 12 (1979), pp. 111-113.

Buchanan, R.H., 'Landscape', Chapter 12 in Northern Ireland, Environment and Natural Resources, (Eds.) J.G. Cruickshank and D.N. Wilcock, Belfast, 1982, pp. 265-289.

Countryside Commission, New Agricultural Landscapes, Cheltenham, 1977.

Countryside Commission for Scotland, Scotland's Scenic Heritage, Battleby, 1978.

Crowe, S. and Miller, Z., (Eds.) Shaping Tomorrow's Landscape, Amsterdam, 1964.

Duffy, P.J., 'Rural Settlement Change in the Republic of Ireland - a Preliminary Discussion' in Geoforum, 14, 2 (1983), pp. 185-191.

Fairbrother, N., New Lives, New Landscapes, Harmondsworth, 1972.

Fehan, J., The Landscape of Slieve Bloom, Dublin, 1979.

Gailey, A., Rural Houses of the North of Ireland, Edinburgh, 1984 (Especially Chapter II).

Green, B.R., 'The Future of the British Countryside', Landscape Planning, 2 (1975), pp. 179-195.

Kennedy, J.J.,and McCusker, P., 'State Forest Amenity Policies for a Growing Urban Irish Population', Chapter 16 in Promise and Performance, Irish Environmental Policies Analysed, (Eds.) J. Blackwell and P.J. Convery, Dublin, 1983, pp. 219-228.

Mawhinney, K.A., 'Recreation', Chapter 10 in Irish Resources and Land Use (Ed.) D.A. Gillmor, Dublin, 1979, pp. 196-225.

Millman, R. and Brandon, P.F., (Eds.) Historical Landscapes : Identification, Recording and Management, 1978 ; Recording Historic Landscapes, 1980; The Threat to the Historic Rural Landscape, 1981. Occasional Papers, Dept. of Geography, Polytechnic of North London.

Mitchell, G.F., The Irish Landscape, London, 1976.

Nelson, C., and Brady, A., <u>Irish Gardening and Horticulture</u>, Royal Horticultural Society of Ireland, 1979.

Newby, P.T., 'Towards an Understanding of Landscape Quality', in <u>Landscape Research</u>, 4 (1979), pp. 11-17.

Niggemann, J., 'The Development of Agrarian Structure and Cultural Landscape', Chapter 6 in <u>Federal Republic of Germany, Spatial Development and Problems</u>, (Eds.) P. Scholler, W. Puls and H.J. Buchholz, Schoningh Paderborn, 1980, pp. 61-66.

Reeves-Smyth, T. and Hamond, F., <u>Landscape Archaeology in Ireland</u>, B.A.R. British Series 116, 1983.

Royal Society of Antiquaries of Ireland, <u>Monuments in Danger</u>, 1983.

Schuyf, J., 'Recording and Management of Historic Landscapes in the Netherlands', Chapter 14 in <u>Historic Landscapes, Identification, Recording and Management</u>, op. cit., 1978.

Shoard, M., 'Why Landscapes are Harder to Protect than Buildings', Chapter 5 in <u>Our Past Before Us. Why Do We Save It</u>, (Eds.) D. Lowenthal and M. Binney, London, 1981.

van Eck, H., et al., <u>Irish Bogs. A Case for Planning</u>, Nijmegen, 1984.

von Kurten, W., 'Landscape Preservation and Landscape Management', Chapter 9 in <u>Federal Republic of Germany, Spatial Development and Problems</u>, op. cit. 1980.

TRADITIONAL BUILDINGS IN THE LANDSCAPE : CONSERVATION AND PRESERVATION

Alan Gailey

Most landscape artifacts, like roads, bridges, reservoirs, field
boundaries, and others suggest human activity in their construction and use, but they may occupy environments largely empty of
people. Ireland does not have extensive 'empty' areas, and man
has rightly been recognised as a major factor in the creation of
parts of the so-called 'natural' landscape of woodland, moor and
bog. It is valid, however, to distinguish buildings from the other
landscape artifacts, for they most obviously imply continuing human
presence.

The functional range of buildings is enormous, as expansive
as man's activities themselves. Nor are buildings randomly distributed in the landscape. Distinctive and much-studied settlement
patterns are the necessary context within which individual
structures are to be fully understood. Planners, geographers, social
historians, and other students of environment may consider these
to be self-evident facts, the accepted base upon which other considerations rest. Yet the settlement context has seldom been
given adequate consideration in conservation and preservation
policies for buildings, alongside architectural and aesthetic
dimensions. Northern Ireland's historic buildings legislation,
for example, is too architecturally based, taking account of
buildings but allowing inadequate consideration to be paid to

their settings. Definition of limited curtilages allows road planners contemplate intruding new lines of carriageway through the rightful settings of important buildings, even between a 'big house' and its gate lodge. While the architectural creations in a great estate like Castleward in county Down can be protected, the same legislation does little for the architecturally landscaped grounds of which the buildings are an integral part.

This paper is based on discussion of the conservation and preservation of rural traditional houses mostly in Northern Ireland. Little has been achieved in this regard elsewhere in Ireland, although there are fundamental features common to the vernacular aspects of the built environment throughout the island. Discussion is limited to rural houses since they provide a manageable body of material, and because other rural building types are yet inadequately understood throughout Ireland. Furthermore, study of urban vernacular housing has hardly commenced; there is still only a single adequate study of the urban vernacular houses of one town (Robinson, 1979).

World-wide cross-cultural study demonstrates that the house is above all a culturally determined form. Its design everywhere owes more to social determinants than to the possibilities and constraints of the physical environment (Rapoport, 1969). This should be remembered when adaptation of certain roof forms and thatching techniques in western and northern coastal Ireland is attributed to response to exposure to Atlantic gales. The house, its form and setting, say much about the nature of society, past and present, and the grounds for urging the preservation of houses in the landscape are not solely architectural and aesthetic, but there is a considerable social history justification also.

Like the landscape itself, buildings are historical 'documents',
to be appreciated as such, as much as for their aesthetic
quality.

A problem and a dilemma arise in the restoration of an old
house. The problem is for society at large, in terms of what the
preserved house represents of past social realities. As time goes
on and all around the house changes, it becomes increasingly
anachronistic, if only because it is an inadequate sample of the
whole of the past. The dilemma for the owner is that the house
will probably have undergone a variety of changes during its
existence. It may have been enlarged, reroofed in a new material,
had its facade remodelled to suit changing fashion. In restoring
it, to what stage does the owner take it back ? To do anything to it is to destroy historical evidence, much as the
archaeologist does by excavating his site; to do nothing may be, at
least potentially, to lose it. Each owner finds his own answer;
in appreciating the preserved house, what has been lost must be
considered as well as what has been saved. A house is akin to
a living organism, and to survive it must be adapted to changing
social circumstances. A successful policy for conservation and
preservation must recognise this; the design challenge for the
architect is therefore enormous, in finding the right balance
between preservation of the heritage of the past, and adaptation
to accommmodate continued occupancy.

Added to these practical considerations of conservation
and preservation of rural housing is the fact that there has
yet been insufficient study of rural vernacular dwellings
throughout Ireland. Pioneering work in all areas since the 1930s
has identified the variety of forms of the single-storey thatched

a

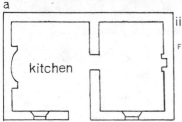

kitchen

Fig. 1. Examples of two fundamental rural vernacular house types.
(a) Direct-entry type fisherman's cottage, Ballycopeland,
Co. Down - (i) elevation, (ii) ground plan, not to scale.
(b) Hearth-lobby farmhouse, for a time the home of the 19th-
century novelist William Carleton, Springtown, Co. Tyrone -
(i) elevation, (ii) ground plan, not to scale.

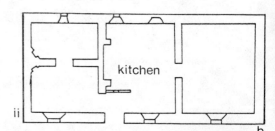

kitchen

Fig. 2. Examples of enlarged and elaborated rural vernacular houses.
(a) Farmhouse of direct-entry type, Terrydreen, Co. Londonderry.
(b) Hearth-lobby farmhouse, two rooms down, two up, Cargaghbane,
Co. Monaghan.

house (a summary is in Gailey, 1984, pp. 10-14) (Fig.1). The view has been expressed that consequently all that needs to be known is on record and that, by implication, everything between these basic forms at one end of the architectural continuum, and the creations of formal design at the other end, is beneath consideration. In Northern Ireland, since about 1970 two circumstances have converged to illustrate this is not the case. Implementation of a statutory listing procedure backed by grant aid, under the Planning (Northern Ireland) Order, 1972 has been based upon necessary field survey, during which many significant houses in rural areas, often aesthetically very pleasing ones, have been identified in this middle ground. Also, the necessary basis of fieldwork to determine a representative collection of vernacular buildings for Ulster's folk museum has extended study to house forms not previously recorded in archives or in published studies (Gailey, 1976a, pp. 54-71; idem, 1984). It is now clear that the basic forms of thatched single-storey houses are just that, and that they were the progenitors of en-larged, elaborated forms which became widespread especially in the second half of the nineteenth century, in response to changing social needs. These developed forms are just as vernacular in character and inspiration as the basic thatched houses themselves (Fig.2). There has emerged also the need to set aside a definition of 'vernacular' that is too dependent on construction using local materials. They were used in the past because it was most economic to do so, not because builders and owners strove to adhere to some mystical association with the local physical environment. More affluent people have long been able to divorce their building activities from dependence on the local environment. As affluence filtered down the social structure more recently, and as economic constraints loosened, particularly as transport networks developed, so dependence of house building on locally available materials diminished. Consideration of house forms, especially of plan types, however, reveals that vernacular attitudes to house design and its development persisted until well within the present century. Indeed, in some cases vernacular design has recently been reworked within the constraints of modern planning requirements, just as it was reworked to produce some of the standardised plans used in building the rural labourers' cottages of the early 1900s.

Where, then, does this enlarged definition of the nature of the vernacular house leave conservation and preservation ? More recent slated, two-storey farm houses are as deserving of attention as smaller thatched ones. If there are those who would deride many of them on aesthetic grounds, it is prudent to recognise that taste in the visual arts is fickle. Only a few generations ago the same thatched houses now commonly regarded as well fitted to the Irish landscape, were the subject of much adverse comment.

Three major areas must be considered in conservation and preservation of rural vernacular housing: history, aesthetics and practicalities. The remainder of this paper deals with a few aspects of each.

HISTORY

The nature of the built environment in former times poses considerable problems in understanding what survives, and what we preserve, of the past. Significant change in building materials used in house construction is well documented in the seventeenth century in many parts of Ireland, from use of wattle and sod, to more load-bearing materials like stone, and even brick in limited districts. In the early seventeenth century only the upper classes lived in dwellings constructed of the more permanent materials. These are the buildings that survive, so understanding the realities of life for the bulk of the population of that time is difficult. At all times wealthier people built more substantial, more permanent homes, and most of the houses now deemed worthy of preservation are from these upper social levels, whether they are the 'big houses' of the landed gentry, or the more modest, but still often well-designed Georgian farmhouses that are such a feature of the Irish landscape from the late eighteenth and early nineteenth centuries.

Well-known historical sources of the early nineteenth century suggest improvement in rural housing in many parts of Ireland (Cullen, 1972, p. 116). The evidence involves qualitative statements which can be difficult to evaluate. A quantitative measure of the extent to which such housing improvement may have progressed is available from data gathered in a remarkable series of statistical surveys of estates carried out in the 1840s (Gailey, 1985; northern data are in idem, 1984, passim). Undoubtedly there were major regional variations in rural housing standards in the 1840s. A county Down estate involved, that of the Marquis of Londonderry about Newtownards and Comber, obviously enjoyed better conditions than, for example, a small north Clare estate at Ballyvaughan. Nevertheless, the overriding conclusion is of the dominance everywhere of the one-storey thatched house of two or three rooms, often with windowless facade, while the 1841 census also testifies to the prevalence of one-room houses in many areas (Ó Danachair, 1967; Gailey, 1976b). Social changes consequent upon the Great Famine

led to the disappearance of most of the poorest houses in rural
Ireland, one-room houses going remarkably rapidly. By the end of the
nineteenth century while two-room houses survived in many districts,
rural houses were predominantly of three or four rooms, and many of
the latter were of two storeys, with two rooms down and two up (Fig.2).
In arguing for preservation of single-storey thatched houses in the
landscape it must be recognised that those which survive mainly
reflect late nineteenth-century conditions, or at best they are a
socially unrepresentative sample from earlier times. If part of the
justification for preserving older houses is that they are part of the
heritage, the incompleteness of the historical record they represent
must also be recognised. Outside a museum, preservation of one-room
houses with mud floors cannot be justified, and to that extent the
physical reality of living conditions only four or five generations
ago is lost.

Another aspect of the historical problem is posed by preservation of older houses. They were integral parts of settlement patterns
now largely disappeared in many areas. Some belonged in small clustered settlements of farms with their outbuildings, often but not
always associated with various forms of open-field farming which often
survived in the nineteenth century only in fossilised forms. Again,
as the road network improved from the late eighteenth century onwards,
roadside sites became more attractive for newer houses, often leading
to dispersal of older house clusters. Such circumstances are the
proper context for understanding survivals of older houses in the
siting of which there are, too, less commonly recognised nuances.
Those that remained farther back from the roadsides often retained
older, open-plan traditional internal arrangements, and less specialised functional differentiation of internal space. Those at the

32

roadsides, in their internal space use, and in increasing external symmetry disguising their internal arrangements, apparently sought to distance themselves from the community at large socially, paradoxically just when they were seeming to get closer to it by moving to the roadsides (Glassie, 1982, chapters 13 and 24; Gailey, 1984, chapter 9). Houses built in either of these ways and changed little over later generations pose fewer problems for the conservationist than those that attempted to change in tune with developing social attitudes. In restoring the latter, should an attempt be made to revert to the old architecturally reflected community openness, recognising that this approach may be out of tune with a changed landscape and settlement pattern in which the house must remain, or should all later alterations be retained some of which may have aesthetic consequences disliked by current fashion, for example in the nature and arrangement of facade openings?

AESTHETICS

The look of a house, and its appearance in the landscape, are contentious matters. An appeal to the past can be counter-productive in achieving an acceptable outcome when alterations are proposed. Many single-storey thatched houses in the early nineteenth century had either no windows, or only a few very small ones in their facades, in explanation of which rural poverty and the cost of window glass were significant factors. What is now often regarded as an acceptable balance between mass and void in the facades of vernacular houses was the outcome of greater affluence, either because in earlier periods there was another source of family income aside from farming, perhaps a craft like weaving, or because such houses were built only as lately as the second half of the nineteenth century. Given such a contrast,

33

it is harder to argue against the introduction of horizontally dominant picture windows, or extended vertical windows with top-hung vents. The external aesthetic consideration has also to be set alongside the internal modern desirability of better natural lighting. However, by addressing the full repertoire of vernacular and historic window and door types, acceptable answers can often be found, for example in the pairing of windows as has been successfully done in some urban neo-vernacular houses in Ulster in recent years in Northern Ireland Housing Executive developments. To achieve the aesthetic requirement in preservation, there may therefore have to be sacrifice of historical fidelity to the past; conservation becomes a matter of architectural spirit rather than faithful preservation of past detail, which may sometimes only be possible in a museum context, if older houses are to continue to be socially acceptable as places for modern people to live.

Other serious problems make even this approach difficult. Many modern materials intended to reduce maintenance costs are inconsistent with any sensible approach to conservation and preservation. The obvious ones are plastics and some kinds of double glazing. Hardwood frames for doors and windows are currently much liked because they may not need frequent repainting. If used in historic architecture to replace older woods which have rotted, sometimes merely due to lack of maintenance, they must be painted to look correct, setting at naught an essential reason for using the modern hardwood frames in the first place. Modern geometrically precise cement rendering, and self-coloured limestone chips, wall finishes intended to minimise maintenance, fundamentally alter the appearance of old houses formerly rendered with uneven plaster or simply repeatedly lime-washed, through which the texture of underlying stonework may show. Cost of materials as much

as of subsequent maintenance, may be a very significant factor.
Asbestos slates, whether of older bland appearance, or some of the
newer textured forms, never repeat the textural and tonal nuances of
natural slate. The visual impact of asbestos slate is immediately
obvious in the Ulster countryside and towns: geometrically precise,
shiny, cheap roofs are everywhere; and they keep the wet out. It is
instructive to take the ferry to Stranraer and within the day travel
through the towns and countryside of south-west Scotland, where
natural slate has been more completely retained. Is it only a
matter of cost that has led to widespread adoption of asbestos slate
in Northern Ireland? Attitudes, and sympathy for the visual quality
of the built environment amongst owners, local legislators, and
planning personnel are crucial factors.

How buildings look in their environment is also important. Why
are certain house forms regarded as acceptable in the landscape, and
others as obtrusive? As in the case of house form, the determinants
are cultural, and as experience broadens with modern opportunities
for travel, ideas from a variety of cultures will inevitably be
mixed in given landscapes. Should this be prevented? In the seventeenth century one of the house forms now regarded as 'traditional'
in rural Ireland was introduced from outside, by settlers from
another land, certainly in the north (Gailey, 1984, pp. 164-188).
Reasons why some houses are seen as acceptable and others not, have
never been adequately studied in Ireland. Living in a society where
the traditional constraints of vernacular design were generally
accepted (for example, an unwillingness to be seen to differ from
one's neighbour), the problem of the acceptability of rural housing
in the landscape did not arise. The legacy of buildings from such
circumstances is now viewed by people living in a new and altered

social enviornment. Major technical changes are also involved. Planners must consider accessibility to services like water and drainage, and the visual problems posed by overhead electricity supplies.

Nevertheless, many people recognise that some constraints should be placed on rural building development if the quality of life for all is to be preserved in the longer term. Inadequately controlled siting of modern housing and its design, and in the past of holiday chalets in north and west Donegal, will diminish the basis of long-term successful tourism. The same is seen in parts of Connemara, and although the problem at first sight seems less severe there at present, these trends are now in evidence in the Dingle peninsula. Rural planning controls have been stricter in recent times in Northern Ireland. A recent, informed north American guest who is an avid student and teacher of Irish history at university level, in conversation with the writer has contrasted the resultant landscapes north and south of the border to the discredit of the latter. Yet to a degree it has been necessary to relax controls on the building of new houses in the Ulster country-side. Relaxation was not opposed by the conservation lobby, for there had been excessive growth about some of the older country towns and villages which consequently were losing much of their historic character. However in permitting new rural housing on sites where historically there had been dwellings, remains of which survive, constraint is still applied in areas of special control, insofar as new houses may not exceed the sizes of the older houses they replace by more than ten per cent.

The relationship between farmhouses, old or new, and their associated farm buildings is more difficult to cope with. Economic

modern farming demands buildings of a scale different from those
of even a generation ago. Farm buildings are usually subject to
only minimal controls, yet they are now the most obtrusive element
in the landscape, especially given some colourings produced by
paint manufacturers. A farmyard develops over time by means of
new buildings added, and old ones replaced by others of quite
different scale, and usually the process is piece-meal over an
extended time-span. The older visually acceptable relationship of
farmhouses and outbuildings may be so totally destroyed that, in
one case in the Mourne area of south Down, listed building consent
for demolition had to be granted some years ago to the owner of an
almost unique vernacular thatched house in that area. The existence
of a statutory listing scheme backed by grant aid does not ensure
preservation in every case, nor is it necessarily arguable that it
should. Furthermore, in Northern Ireland, controls on rural housing
development were exercised in another way, even before the advent of
statutory listing. The Ulster Countryside Committee set guidelines,
including encouragement of buildings of relatively low profile in
the landscape, to try to accord with older vernacular norms, advising
pitched roofs with whitewashed walls.

PRACTICALITIES

Sufficient has already been indicated of legislation on conservation
and preservation of buildings on grounds of their architectural or
historic merit to indicate that Northern Ireland enjoys an apparently
more advantageous situation than the rest of the island. That
historic buildings legislation must be seen, however, in a wider
administrative and legislative context, dealing with more general
environmental matters. The potential of having all planning and

conservation matters dealt with in a single Department of the
Environment has yet to be fully realised. Lack of sympathy for,
even understanding of conservation in some levels of administration
militates against fully effective action. The basis for a stronger
administrative voice to be given to the conservation interest is
advocated in the recent Balfour Report, which recommends structural
changes in Northern Ireland's Department of the Enviornment
(Balfour, 1984). The report proposes that countryside and buildings
conservation should have equally effective voices at sufficiently
high levels to demand fuller consideration independently of more
general planning and development interests within the town and
country planning service in the same Department.

Northern Ireland's historic buildings legislation became
effective only in 1972, since when about three-quarters of a potentially listable 8000+ buildings have been recommended to the
Department of the Environment by the Historic Buildings Council for
statutory listing. Inevitably most of these listed buildings are
from the formal end of the architectural continuum; but from the
beginning significant numbers of rural vernacular houses have been
listed. This is important in an architecturally modest built environment like Northern Ireland's. Members of the Historic Buildings
Council are impatient with recent slowing down of listing, due to
manning difficulties in the Department of the Environment and have
pressed the minister concerned to relieve the situation; some
staffing relief is now to be provided. Other changes are needed,
in the light of experience. The excessively architectural basis
of the legislation has been commented on already. Powers included
in the historic buildings legislation in Britain, on which Northern
Ireland's was modelled, are missing, particularly so far as

compulsory repairs are concerned. If an owner has a mind to do so, he may simply allow a valuable listed property to disintegrate through neglect. Other problems in the legislation relate to diff- iculties experienced in the small number of conservation areas, which are dominantly urban.

The historic buildings legislation rests on a stick-and- carrot basis, the stick being restriction of an owner's freedom of action, the carrot being grant aid towards restoration and conserv- ation work. The sums disbursed annually are not small. Details of some 1100 grant cases completed in the first ten years, since 1973, are set out in a recent publication (Pierce, Coey and Oram, 1984). So far as traditional rural houses are concerned, occasionally and particularly when dealing with thatch, extremely generous grants have been made available, and given that thatch presents a continuing maintenance problem, the need for ongoing assistance is recognised. Hopefully in this way a modest number of traditional thatched houses can be preserved spread throughout Northern Ireland. To this end a greater number are listed, for as already demonstrated in one case from south Down, not all will survive. Numbers of other types of vernacular housing, one- and two-storeyed with slate roofs, are also being listed and when necessary grant-aided. As important as the grant-aid element of this procedure is the fact that owners of vernacular rural houses are of necessity confronted with specialist advice on how to conserve or restore their homes. Perhaps in the long term this educative dimension of the listing process will be the most important. In these early stages, however, the struggle often seems uphill. Owners are only slowly becoming aware of the ultimate advantages of having listed buildings. A minority have been greatly pleased in the end, having been prevailed upon to

adopt renovation procedures they initially regarded as unnecessary.
Estate agents now occasionally advertise statutory listing of a
property as an asset. Example to be followed is gradually exerting
an influence; this is already most marked in one or two of the
conservation areas, and good results are now being seen in both
Hillsborough and Portaferry in county Down, the outcome of persuas-
iveness by committed conservationists, including officials of the
Historic Buildings Branch of the Department of the Environment.

A greater educational task is involved, of the community at
large and not just the owners of listed properties. A considerable
problem is the absence of good design training in general education
in Ireland. This manifests itself in attitudes displayed by
individuals in positions of influence, for example amongst planning
officers trained as sociologists or geographers having no architectural design background. Planning appeals commissioners have been
known to fail to appreciate why it is necessary to retain natural
slate and have allowed appeals demanding asbestos-covered roofs.

Yet it must be acknowledged there are severe practical
problems to be overcome in conserving, restoring and preserving
traditional houses in the landscape. Matters relating to external
appearance have been identified. Given the limited accommodation
in so many traditional houses, there are design problems in bringing
them up to acceptable modern standards, even when waivers can be
granted under building regulations to retain their historic character.
Unless grant-aid going beyond usual limits is available, it can be
difficult to persuade an owner that he must spend additional money
in providing a rear extension with a pitched roof when a flat one
is cheaper (that a flat roof may, in the long term, generate maintenance problems, seems to carry little weight). A desire to force

more use into a roof space than it can accommodate without enormous protrusions of unsympathetically proportioned dormer windows is difficult to overcome. In the end, the problems of updating older traditional houses in rural areas can be overcome, but they demand appreciation of the vernacular repertoire of constructional and design elements included in rural housing of the past. Those best equipped to resolve the problems are those with formal training in handling design problems, and not one's friends down the road who know how to draw a plan adequately to pass through planning and building control procedures. The relationship between a client and his consultant is delicate, but there has to be a greater persuasive role for the architect than appears presently to be manifested.

The subject of overall context must be raised again. If in persuading owners to adopt conservation-oriented attitudes to their older property, design as a factor in the overall planning context of rural areas is ignored, conservation in general is ill-served, and those owners of architecturally and historically significant properties will be left without a setting sympathetic to their efforts. Rural Ireland has not been best served by the architectural profession thus far. Some parts of Europe have been able to develop contemporary vernacular housing drawing on the experience of the past; examples may be seen in Brittany. Having made this criticism in a recent book (Gailey, 1984, p. 242), the writer was taken to task by a well-known reviewer for failing to recognise the contribution of Northern Ireland Housing Executive development architects (Brett, 1984). Their recent achievements are undoubtedly very significant; but these achievements have been in the cities and towns, not in the countryside which was the concern of the book at issue. Looking around the rural landscape in Ireland, one is struck by the insidious

imposition of architecturally dismembered suburbia across the
countryside. The greatly enhanced mobility that modern transport
provides means that not only can the suburbanite live in the country,
in his mass-produced house, but the emulation of the suburbanite by
the genuinely rural dweller is thereby encouraged, as if attitudes
propagated by the media were not enough to contend with, in these
days of international communication. There is great need for good
modern design in housing sympathetic to the rural landscape in
which the past is a more pervasive element than in the suburbs, to
counter what some years ago was described as the 'bungalisation' of
the countryside (Gailey, 1977, footnote); that awkward word conveys
a sense of an inappropriate house type, as well as a realisation of
the lack of concern of society generally for its environment.

CONCLUSION

If much of what this paper advances seems pessimistic or negative,
such is not its purpose. In seeking a way forward, it is best to
be fully aware of the problems and the difficulties. The second
of the objectives set before contributors to this symposium must
now be addressed: steps which might be taken to conserve and if
possible enhance landscape quality. Three paths amongst others
contribute to a way forward. The first is educational. Society
in general and owners of relevant properties in particular, have
to be convinced that conservation attitudes need to be applied to
the countryside. Architecturally good work is already being done.
There have been surveys of the architectural heritage of Irish
towns, whether sponsored by An foras Forbartha or by the Ulster
Architectural Heritage Society. What is wrong with these is that
they are presently concentrated on urban areas, where the most

extensive groupings of formal architectural achievement may be
expected. This survey work must be extended to rural areas and to
traditional buildings, and its outcome disseminated, by whatever
means, throughout the population at large. There is no long-term
future in restricting its outcome to conservation organisations;
that is only to preach to the converted. Recent attempts by the
Ulster Architectural Heritage Society to spread conservation ideals
more widely, for example to schools, are commendable. Governmental
agencies have a role to play. The outcome of statutory listing and
the designation of conservation areas in Northern Ireland needs to
be publicised more than is being done at present. Recent publication
of Taken for Granted, a record of the first ten years' implementation
of statutory listing and grant aid in Northern Ireland must only be
a start, if environmental conservation, including the built environment, rural and urban, is to be effective.

Secondly, society must be prepared to spend resources on
conservation. If owners of properties of historic or architectural
merit are to recognise that they are keepers of a heritage for
society generally, then society has a responsibility to help them
to maintain that heritage. Not to recognise this, yet to argue
that conservation is necessary and a good thing, is to lack realism.
Creation of the formal structures for such support presupposes a
climate of opinion in which those structures can be accepted and in
which they will thrive in years to come. Again, the importance of
education at all levels from primary school to preparation for, and
enjoyment of, leisure in retirement cannot be minimised.

Lastly, the design profession, especially architects, must
take greater responsibility for the future, than merely to give in
to clients who can only argue from the standpoint of their own

experience. Likewise, if there is to be valid conservation of the
countryside, then architectural design must recognise the nature of
what has gone before, and greater effort must be expended on study
of the full reality of the vernacular built environment than has
yet been in evidence. It is simply not true that all the old traditional houses are gone and that nothing remains to be recorded.
New design building upon the vernacular tradition is more likely to
provide buildings at home in the landscape, in contrast to the
awkwardness of most of the new rural houses built in Ireland in the
last generation.

If what is happening in Northern Ireland in environmental
conservation of buildings seems rather more adequate than in the
rest of Ireland, a comparative perspective is helpful. Historic
buildings legislation in the north only nibbles at the edges of what
is really required. 8000 or more potentially listable buildings in
Northern Ireland may seem impressive; this figure is less than the
total number of listed buildings in the city of Bath and its surrounding district. Some thirty conservation areas are presently
anticipated, the most recently designated being Downpatrick; England
alone has 5500. If these figures serve to underline the unpretent-
iousness of Northern Ireland's built environment, then surely
consideration afforded to the vernacular aspect of that environment
is all the more essential, to secure the influence of yesterday's
rural heritage for the landscape of tomorrow.

REFERENCES

Balfour, Jean, A New Look at the Northern Ireland Countryside,
          H.M.S.O., Belfast, 1984.

Brett, C.E.B., Review of Rural Houses of the North of Ireland, in
          Belfast Telegraph, 4 Aug. 1984.

Cullen, L.M., Economic History of Ireland since 1660, London, 1972.

Ó Danachair, C., 'The Bothan Scóir' in Rynne E. (ed.), North Munster
          Studies. Essays in Memory of Rev. M.J. Moloney,
          Limerick, 1967.

Gailey, A., 'Local Life in Ulster 1843-1848: The Statistical Surveys
          of Maurice Collis' in Ulster Local Studies, 9, No. 20
          (1985), pp. 120-127.

idem, Rural Houses of the North of Ireland, Edinburgh, 1984.

idem, 'Vernacular Dwellings of Clogher Diocese' in Clogher Record, 9,
          2 (1977), pp. 187-231.

idem, 'Some Developments and Adaptations of Traditional House Types'
          in Ó Danachair, C. (ed.), Folk and Farm. Essays in Honour of
          A.T. Lucas, Dublin, 1976a, pp. 54-71.

idem, 'The Housing of the Rural Poor in Nineteenth-Century Ulster' in
          Ulster Folklife, 22 (1976b), pp. 34-57.

Glassie, H., Passing the Time in Ballymenone, Dublin, 1982.

Pierce, R., Coey, A. and Oram, R., Taken for Granted, Belfast, 1984.

Rapoport, A., House Form and Culture, Englewood Cliffs, 1969.

Robinson, P., 'Urban Vernacular Housing in Newtownards, County Down'
          in Folk Life, 17 (1979), pp. 1-28.

NEW FARM BUILDINGS

P.J. Tuite

INTRODUCTION

Open-countryside occupies 98 per cent of the surface of Ireland, only
2 per cent being covered by built up areas. While there are numerous
other agencies at work in rural areas, the major portion of our landscape is in the keeping of 16 per cent of our population, the farming
community. Ireland has an infinite variety of landscape, fields, forest,
mountains, beaches all within short distances from our urban areas, so,
that it is possible for the modern city dweller to use them at week-
ends because of his newly acquired mobility. Some areas receive no
visitors, except in summer, and some, mainly beauty spots, have more
visitors than residents, and being in a majority they are apt to forget that there are people who must live in the country all the year
round. The urbanite sees the country as a recreation ground where,
incidentially, food is produced and vaguely he wishes to preserve what
he enjoys, forgetting that the country is a living and changing organism
and much of what he finds attractive is man made and not natural. Without the constant attention of the farming community our country would
revert to its natural state and the farmers render, however unconsciously,
a service to the whole community which has an indefinable value. The
farmer however, sees the country differently. Land is to him a resource
to be exploited in the pursuit of his livelihood and although he may be
sensitive to his surroundings he is not opposed to altering them as
economic dictate. His task is not an easy one. The evolution of
agriculture in the 20th century has resulted in important developments
in the character and layout of farm buildings and farms themselves.
Mechanisation and the application of scientific research are transforming

Fig I   Farm buildings today are industrial in origin

agriculture into a highly complex industry. World competition makes
it particularly important that our agriculture should be as effective
as possible, and that means that there must be efficient buildings as
well as efficient machines.

The major change which will be brought about by economic pressures
will be a change of scale. Farm buildings are seen as part of the
familiar countryside pattern of houses, trees and fields and the
observer becomes accustomed to a range of relative sizes usual to the
area. Scale in this context means the relationship in size between
objects, natural and man made, in the landscape. Until recently the
pattern of farming has been on a small scale and the buildings have
been largely inconspicuous because of their limited size and traditional materials. Just as the scale of our towns is changing with
larger and taller buildings, so big structures are becoming features of
the countryside. Major roads, power stations, electric pylons,
factory chimneys and cooling towers are more in evidence. Farming is
also changing its scale of operations and needs bigger units, bigger
fields, more especially bigger buildings to house more activity under
cover. The buildings become dominant, rather than casual incidents
in the landscape. This change in scale is posed by modern needs. The
aim should be to accept the challenge and make the best of the new, not
to oppose progress because it involves unfamiliar problems.

The raw materials of farm building design

Traditional farm buildings are characterised by the directness both in
the way materials were used and in the way the buildings were planned.
For the most part the materials used were found locally - stone, wood,
clay, straw, roads and slates and they received little modifications
before they were assembled. Crude and primitive though these buildings
may seem they have stront characteristics which connect them to the land

47

and to the landscape but with the replacement of these traditional
materials and methods the vernacular spirit has died and its return
is impossible because local materials have become a luxury product and
the local crafts have died. In contrast, the buildings of today are
constructed of materials of little intrinsic beauty but nevertheless
it is with such inexpensive and unpretentious materials that we must
continue to build, since more pleasing alternatives would increase
costs and any advice on their use would be ignored. Galvanised steel,
asbestos cement, plaster and concrete are naturally light in colour and
therefore conspicuous and their successful treatment requires skill in
design. Mention must also be made of the range of standard steel frame
buildings clad in either corrugated steel or corrugated asbestos. These
buildings are serviceable, low in cost and acceptable to the farmers,
and are now in widespread use throughout the country. Over the years
the roof spans available have increased enormously and we are now well
into the age of the large span building. The sheeting habitually used
for cladding farm buildings are corrugated in profile and it is
indicitive of an indifferent if not of a negative attitude to design,
that the same profile should be used indiscriminately for every sheeted
surface rather than different profiles for roof sheeting and for wall
sheeting, because the protection required and the stresses are different.
Thus an opportunity to articulate the general form of the building in
a rational manner is lost and no practical advantage is gained. It is
a cardinal principle of design that each element of a building should
have a character expressive of its function, as part of the building.

In the handling of new materials, I must deplore the practice of attempting to conceal their nature by simulating older and more expensive forms, which is never successful. Plastering, scored with lines can never resemble brick work, nor textured concrete pass for stone, and such dishonesty fools nobody.

Colour

The application of colour can do much to enhance simple materials but colour in farm buildings is treated with an extraordinary lack of skill and thought. Recently I received a sample of sheet steel produced specially for agricultural buildings which was a bright green colour - allegedly grass green. I find it almost impossible to imagine a situation in the context of agricultural buildings where this colour would be suitable. Its choice stems from the misconception that by painting something the same colour as its background, it will disappear. This is erroneous because texture, shape and shadow content are much more important factors in questions of concealment than colour. This attitude to colour is negative and stems from a lack of understanding of the principles involved in the use of colour. Let it be clearly understood that concealment by the use of colour alone is impossible. Besides, all buildings in the countryside need not necessarily recede into the landscape, and if they are clean and simple in outline, there is no good reason why a suitable contrast could not be the aim. The most pleasing combination of colours, to be seen at present, in the countryside has been introduced unconsciously into farm buildings, with their dark red oxide painted roofs, white-washed walls and black tarred plinths.

Before selecting materials and colour for an agricultural building, it must first be decided whether it is to be a positive or negative element in its surroundings. As a general rule darker colours tend to

Fig 2. Light coloured sheet materials make buildings conspicuous

be negative in their effect and light colours positive. Also, it is worth remembering that any natural colour - that is colour that is found in nature - will be more in harmony in a natural setting than a colour devised by a paint manufacturer.

Texture

Texture is a more difficult factor to discuss. At a distance a smooth surface, even if painted black, will under certain conditions of light, look white. The only way to control this phenomena is to make the surface rough or textured.

Most sheet materials have a textured quality built into them by the corrugations which give them rigidity. By using a different pattern of sheeting for the wall surface, from that used on the roof, the shape of the building can be better defined. It should be remembered, however, that from a few hundred yards distance one cannot different-iate between one pattern of corrugation and another in sheets of the same material, and colour. The juxta position of materials of widely differing natures, such as sheeting, concrete blocks and timber is a far better way of achieving the differentiation of the various parts of a building. Smooth and shiny materials also have a part to play here and aluminium storage bins, grain silos and roofs can often add parts of interest and contrast in an otherwise uninteresting group of buildings.

Siting and layout

While no very startling advances are to be expected in the design of structures for farm buildings, or in their planning, the development of mechanical equipment for handling crops and stock is already having a marked effect on the planning of the complete farm unit. The traditional plan of a farm, had the buildings disposed around a

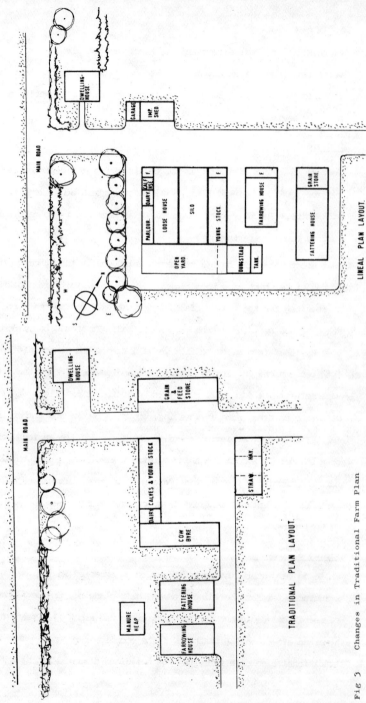

LINEAL PLAN LAYOUT.

MAIN ROAD

DWELLING-HOUSE

GARAGE | IMP SHED

PARLOUR. | DAIRY | CALF HSE | F.
LOOSE HOUSE
SILO
YOUNG STOCK | F.
OPEN YARD
DUNGSTEAD
TANK.
FARROWING HOUSE | F.
FATTENING HOUSE
GRAIN STORE

TRADITIONAL PLAN LAYOUT.

MAIN ROAD.

DWELLING-HOUSE

GRAIN & FEED STORE.

DAIRY CALVES & YOUNG STOCK
COW BYRE
STRAW. HAY.
MANURE HEAP
FATTENING HOUSE
FARROWING HOUSE

Fig 3   Changes in Traditional Farm Plan

rectangular court, often with a dungstead at its centre. Farm work was manual and the short distances between the buildings saved energy, in fact the concentric plan was ideal. The introduction of the tractor and the dependence of farms on road transport for the delivery and removal of feed and products, and more recently the increasing use of mechanical equipment within the buildings has revolutionised the traditional plan.

A wide, well surfaced roadway replaces the farmyard. At one end it connects to the highway and at the other provides access to the fields. Implements and crop products are housed to one side of this road ready for use in the fields, or for collection, and the stock enclosures together with their ancilliary buildings are placed on the other side. Food stores are accessible from loading bays adjacent to the roadway. A loop road encircles the buildings, and the dungstead is sited at a far end of the buildings sufficiently distant away to allow for the linear extension of the stock buildings.

A further factor involves the comfort of workers and livestock, for maximum protection and lighting. Buildings are being preferably sited on hillsides or gentle slopes to obtain dry sites and ease of drainage and where effluents, which might be offensive, can be stored or treated well away from houses. Buildings should be arranged compactly with a minimum of waste space between them.

In the design of farm buildings there is no need for a multiplicity of materials, building shapes, roof pitches or window sizes in one group, not for haphazard and unrelated additions, if sufficient attention is given to the planning and use of adaptable structures. Where factory-made buildings are used in any quantity, they should have a family likeness. Considerably variation in shape, complication in layout, and changes of height can be accepted if the materials used are consistent, particularly the roofing material.

Attention must also be given to the design and the disposition of ancilliary components, such as fences, walls, gates and service roads. A consistant design policy e.g. the use of a standard fence or walling element can have a unifying effect on the group as a whole.

The tidiness of the farm buildings, and of their surroundings is a simple measure of good organisation. The layout and buildings should be designed to simplify maintenance. Fences and paved areas should be designed to avoid corners, difficult to clean and where clutter and scrap may accumulate. Keeping the farm clean, tidy and handsome should become a simple continuing process. The clearing away of the remains of obsolete buildings and equipment is especially important.

In addition, to providing shelter, trees and hedges can play an important part in linking buildings with one another, and with the landscape as a whole. Choice of species in planting should be related to the area. Trees already flourishing in the district will grow better and look better. In many rural areas, the group planting of trees is preferable to single rows in softening the outline of new farm buildings.

Shelter

The use of planting to affort shelter from the wind is so important that it can be deemed essential. Powerful gales can be lifted from the ground by careful planting, far more effectively than by a wall. A wall gives very little shelter in a high wind as the wind curves inwards again almost immediately whereas a good shelter belt can effect a wind reduction on the leeward side for a distance of ten times the height of the trees and it can also raise the ambient temperature by 2°C to 3°F over the same spot unsheltered. In general, shelter belts should be planted at right angles to the prevailing wind - open textured planting filters wind and reduces its force - the broader the belt the more effective the filtering effect. It is most important to combine low and high planting in such a way that the taller plants or trees are adequately protected and that the general outline is streamlined to raise the path of the wind and provide adequate shelter on the leeward side. If good protection is required all the year round, a proportion of evergreen planting is necessary and in any case plant material which has dense twigs should be chosen. Planting needs to be close and upright so that the trees and shrubs form a single unit rather than separate individuals. The optimum density for a shelter belt is between 50% to 60% i.e. 40% to 50% permeable to wind. Thin or open planting is little use and a dense windbreak produces the same effect as a solid wall.

Conclusions

1. In nearly all cases a satisfactory appearance depends not on spending money, but on making wise choices between alternatives. The cumulative effect of the choices made by the farmer and his advisers will determine the appearance of much of our countryside for a long time to come.

2. A building programme can prevent wasteful and untidy alterations and ensure that immediate work helps instead of hinders future changes. The programme cannot be rigid. Buildings must meet functional requirements and be changeable to future demands.

3. The appearance of the farm should be considered as a whole. The design and tidiness of the area around the buildings and the lay-

out of roads and of overhead wires in the vicinity all contribute to create a pleasing landscape.

4. It is a basic requirement that the buildings should meet the technical needs of agriculture in terms of cost and performance and there is also a social responsibility on the part of the farmer and of manufacturers to accept appearance as an essential factor of design.

5. Appearance and performance go hand-in-hand from the beginning. Good looks cannot be added at some stage after the initial design and layout. Good design is not an expensive luxury but can be achieved with little or no additional cost. Basic requirements, common to demands of good farming and amenity, are clean, simple and tidy buildings.

6. The technological revolution is gaining speed and it thus becomes increasingly urgent that the changes in farm buildings which will inevitably result should be so designed and organised, that they enhance, and do not disfigure our countryside. It is imperative that a national policy on the appearance of farm buildings be defined and implemented.

References

Allot, D.J. and Young, 'The appearance of farm buildings in the country-side - the agricultural consideration' in Farm Buildings Digest, 6, 1 (1971), pp. 5-6.

Clarke, P.O., 'The appearance of farm buildings' in The Farm Buildings Association Journal, 12, (1968), pp. 60-65.

Council of Industrial Desing ; Advisory Panel on Farm Buildings. 'Appraisal of the design of tower silos in the landscape' in The Farm Buildings Association Journal, 12, (1968), pp. 67-68.

Fairbrother, N., New Lives, New Landscapes, London, 1970, pp. 7-8.

Ferguson, I.B., 'Changing attitudes to agriculture and farm buildings' in Farm Buildings Progress, 64, (1981), pp. 29-31.

Hardy, A.C., 'The appearance of farm buildings - colour finishes' in Farm Buildings Digest, 6, 1. (1971), pp. 9-10.

Morrison, M.D.C., 'Farm buildings and the future' in Farm Buildings Association Journal, 23, (1978), pp. 19-26.

Rogerson, P.D., 'The disappearance of rural buildings' in Farm Building Progress, 26, (1971), pp. 19-26.

Sayce, R.B., 'Farm buildings in the countryside' in The Farm Buildings Association Journal, 23, (1978), pp. 67-68.

Soutar, D.S. and Ferguson, I.B., 'How to improve the appearance of farm buildings' in Farm Building Progress, 61, (1980), pp. 1-2.

Wallace, D.C., 'Farm buildings in the landscape' in Farm Buildings Digest, 10, 1, (1975), pp. 3-4.

Weller, J.B., 'The appearance of farm buildings - the designer's view' in Farm Building Progress, 6, 1, (1971), pp.7-8.

Westmacott, R. and Worthington, T., New Agricultural Landscapes, The Countryside Commission, (1974), pp. 69-70.

White, J.N., 'Colour finishes for farm buildings' in The Farm Buildings Association Journal, 14, (1970), pp. 11-12.

SETTLEMENT PATTERNS: RURAL HOUSING, VILLAGES, SMALL TOWNS

Patrick Shaffrey

INTRODUCTION

This paper deals essentially with the physical and aesthetic
aspects of both the traditional and emerging rural settlement
pattern, but with particular reference to housing, as opposed to
other rural buildings - churches, schools, shops. Social and
economic aspects are referred to only in as much as they have an
effect on the aesthetic quality of the landscape.

In a rural landscape natural elements are the predominant
visual characteristics - mountains, lakes, rivers, forests, trees
and hedgerows. Rural buildings are generally subservient to this
natural landscape and their essential visual and aesthetic qualities
are created by relationships with the surrounding topography and
natural features. In cities and towns, on the other hand, the
overall character and atmosphere derives mainly from the arrangement of buildings and the spaces they form with each other.

EUROPEAN CONTEXT

Ireland is different from most other European countries in respect
of its rural policies and their effect on the landscape. The
European settlement pattern generally consists of cities, large and
small towns, villages, and farming hamlets, though there are
occasional areas where a more dispersed settlement pattern can be
observed, such as the Brittany coast and some upland regions.
Driving through Wales and England, across France and Switzerland,

Fig. 1. Co. Tyrone – Farm complex nestling within the contours of the landscape.

over the Lombardy Plain and towards Tuscany and Rome, a highly
diverse settlement pattern can be observed, but all held together
by an important common characteristic, namely a clear physical
separation of settlements and countryside. In Ireland, however,
the rural landscape is becoming suburbanised and the visual
distinction between the settlements and the surrounding countryside
increasingly blurred. In certain parts of the country it is
difficult to identify where one village ends and the next begins.
This process, which is a relatively modern phenomenon, is changing
the aesthetic appearance of the lowland countryside. The origin
and consequences of rural suburbanisation are the main concerns of
this paper along with consideration of future policies to protect
the traditional rural landscape. There is also another difference
between ourselves and our European neighbours to be noted, particularly in the small towns and villages. In Ireland there is less
emphasis on local architectural styles, something which is still
clearly evident in other European countries. This problem clearly
merits further consideration but is not dealt with in this paper.

Ireland's overall settlement structure of cities, towns,
villages and hamlets is not basically different from the European
model. But our farming population was, and is, more dispersed.
Farms are small and there is a tradition of living in scattered
farms, rather than in villages or hamlets as in many parts of
Europe. In the past, however, most of the rural population worked
on the farm and their farmsteads fitted snugly into the landscape
and could be seen almost as a part of nature (Fig. 1). The
inhabitants of the modern houses in the countryside today are

rarely involved in farming. Their building requirements are no different from those of the ordinary suburban dweller, as is their general lifestyle. We will return to this central issue after a brief survey of the broad range of settlement patterns, the development of which will affect the rural landscape in some form or other.

SETTLEMENT PATTERNS

Two distinct patterns of rural living can be recognised in Ireland. Firstly, isolated housing and, secondly, the nucleated settlements of varying size, formality and physical definition (Shaffrey, 1985).

Rural Housing

This covers a variety of building types:

(a) Estate Houses

The great landed estates were widely distributed throughout the countryand normally included a substantial mansion and also smaller houses both for the family, relatives and retainers involved in the management of the estate. Although many large houses are gone, significant numbers still remain, and sub-stantially more of the smaller types. They were all subject to a significant design input at the construction stage, and this is still clearly evident today. Their outstanding characteristic is the attractive relationship between the house and heavily planted grounds.

(b) Farms

Farmhouses were the most numerous type of rural dwelling and varied considerably in size and style. Two-storey classical-

Fig. 2.   Near Craughwell, Co. Galway - Classical style country residence.
Fig. 3.   Geashill, Co. Offaly - The high standard of architecture and construction achieved in Estate Villages.

style houses, showing the influence of polite architecture are
numerous on large farms (Fig. 2.) Smaller farmers lived in
simpler single-storey or two-storey houses. The most significant visual aspect of farms is the relationship of the
dwelling house to the out-buildings and the external relationship of the entire group with the surrounding landscape.
There are many variations in the layout of dwelling house and
outbuildings, which exhibit interesting regional characteristics. They are among the more pleasant aesthetic features of
the countryside, but their fine qualities have not yet been
widely recognised, either by Local Authorities, or, more
importantly, by the farming community.

(c) Cottages

The country cottage has a long tradition going back to the
medieval labourers, who lived in huts made of wattle and clay.
The term covers different types. Older cottages were built of
mud and stone, with thatch, slate or iron roofs, and mostly
single storey. County Council cottages have been widely built
since the establishment of the County Councils at the end of
the nineteenth century. The earlier ones are attractive buildings on acre or half acre plots, and generally single or one
and a half storeys. Estate cottages have a more refined architectural expression as befits their relationship with important
estates. Generally they were built of stone with slated roofs
(Fig. 3).
Originally the country cottages were built for people traditionally associated with the countryside - farm labourers and

tradesmen, such as blacksmiths, carpenters, and wheelwrights.
Today, many cottages still remain, though in most instances
the original occupants have gone. The dwelling may have been
extended, not always in the best of taste, and "the acre plot"
is often in a semi-derelict state. Others have, however,
retained their distinctive architectural qualities and rural
characteristics, and exhibit all the charm and quality traditionally associated with rural living.

(d) Modern Rural Housing

This is a new and special type of rural housing, the so-called
"urban-generated housing". Much of it has been built over the
last two decades, and mainly in the form of bungalows, although
recently two-storey houses are becoming more popular. These
new dwellings occur throughout the countryside, but generally
there are more specific concentrations closer to the larger
towns. The owners are people engaged in urban-type activities
- teachers, bank clerks, civil servants, builders, accountants,
and a host of other occupations - nearly all work in nearby
towns.

The new houses have more in common with urban and suburban
buildings than with the traditional building types. They pay
little respect to orientation or topography; they face directly
on to the road, irrespective of views; building techniques and
materials show little regard for local traditions; any existing
planting and vegetation are often cleared straight away leaving
a bare building patch which may take generations to recover.

Nucleated Settlements

There are different types of nuclei, all well distributed, particularly in the lowland areas. The high density of rural population
in the nineteenth century, and the simplicity of transportation
compared with today, required a network of settlements to act as
service/meeting places for the rural population. As a result a
comprehensive network of centres of varying size has developed.
Small villages or hamlets are often within four miles of each other,
with perhaps seven to eight miles between the smaller towns, and
ten to twenty between the larger sized towns, with the regional or
sub-regional capitals thirty to fifty miles apart. The most common
type is the small village or hamlet, and the glaring failure to
grasp the significance and potential of these small settlements in
the context of modern society has been a major weakness of current
planning policies.

The different types of nucleated settlement are as follows:

(a) Clachans

These are groups of farms and cottages clustered together in an
informal manner and lacking shops, a church or any other
institutions. There is a most interesting and historically
significant group of clachans in South Kilkenny, near Waterford
city, including Licketstown, Corluddy, and others. There are
others on the Dingle Peninsula, e.g. Reask, and also on the
Cooley Peninsula in County Louth, where Whitestown is a
prominent example.

The settlement pattern along the western seaboard, especially
in Connemara and West Donegal, can be broadly described within

Fig. 4.   Pleasant atmosphere - typical of Bord na Mona housing schemes.

Fig. 5.   Achill Island - random development but with its own distinctive character.

this category (Fig. 5). However, compared to South Kilkenny
and County Louth, the way of life relates more to subsistence
type farming and fishing, and building form is influenced by
the distinctive topography. The clachans have a striking
visual expression, particularly the traditional buildings
fitting into the rocky landscapes and enlivened by whitewashed
walls, and roofs of slate or thatch.

(b) Crossroads Villages/Hamlets

These settlements contain often nothing more than a shop, a
few farms and cottages and perhaps a church and school, which
enable them to function as local service centres. There is
little formality about their layout, and, in the physical
sense, they are an integral part of the landscape. Such
settlements are dotted all around the countryside. They
rarely have any organised facilities, such as public water or
sewerage, except perhaps when they are close to a large town.
In this situation, however, the hamlet may have lost all its
visual distinctiveness, and its planning and aesthetic problems
are more urban in character.

(c) Agricultural Villages

These settlements generally have a population of less than two
hundred persons. They may contain a mixture of houses, perhaps
one or two farm complexes, a few shops, branch creamery, church,
schools, small workshops. The layout is quite informal, but
the visual expression is significantly stronger than the crossroads village, and they provide a wider range of social
facilities. Many have a piped water supply, but comparatively

few have public sewerage facilities.

(d) Special-Type Villages - Estate, Industrial, Fishing

As their name implies these settlements have specific origins.
The location was predetermined by factors, such as the development of a great estate, the establishment of industry, or a
suitable landing place along the coast. The social importance
of agriculture is not as evident and as a result the settlements
have fewer shops and other commercial facilities than other
villages. However, they generally have a stronger physical
expression, whether in a formal sense, as in estate villages
such as Ardagh, County Longford and Glaslough, County Monaghan,
or a more informal and romantic pattern, as in fishing villages
such as Kilmore Quay, County Wexford.

The villages built by Bord na Mona in the forties and fifties
come into this category. In a town planning and urban design
context they are among the more significant and interesting
developments since the foundation of the State. Good examples
are Doire Dhraighneach, near Rochfordbridge in County Westmeath,
and Coill Dubh in County Kildare. They have been well maintained over the years and fine traditions in this regard have
been established by Bord na Mona (Fig. 4). Even though the
houses are now mostly in private ownership the overall sense
of concern for their presentation and appearance is still
evident.

(e) Small Towns

These generally have a population of between two hundred and
five hundred persons and function essentially as rural service

centres. Their form consists of buildings with mixed uses
along a single street or grouped around a small square. There
are few, if any, other streets of significance. In the past
most towns had a weekly market/fair which the smaller villages
rarely had. Irish towns, because of their important service
function, contain an unusually high number of shops and other
commercial enterprises, as well as a number of significant
public buildings, such as churches, schools, market house.
Towns above five hundred population have a more complex physical
pattern. They are more detached physically from the surrounding landscape, and their planning problems are essentially urban
rather than rural.

HISTORICAL BACKGROUND
There are broadly speaking three different periods within which
human activities have shaped the modern rural landscape.
1690-1850
This was the period of the Great Estates, which were located
throughout the entire lowland countryside. The owners and managers
exercised great influence over a wide range of building ventures
and the countryside was transformed from its wild pristine state of
the sixteenth century to the rural landscape of great houses and
demesnes, which are still an important part of the rural landscape
today. In the early nineteenth century, following a long period
of general economic improvements, the density of rural population
was extremely high and population pressures led to the continuous
sub-division of already inadequate small holdings. F. Mitchell

(1976) has described the Irish countryside at that time as follows: - "The countryside must have presented an extraordinary appearance. There were the walled demesnes with their trees, like oases in a desert. The boughs of the trees hung down over the walls, but inside the walls there were man-traps to deter timber-poachers. There were the farmers' houses surrounded by shelter-belts of trees, and the farmers would have a blunderbuss to protect them. And then there was nothing, not a tree, not a bush, to break the view of the bare landscape dotted over with cabins and endless potato-patches".

1850-1960s

The Great Famine was a watershed. From then until the 1960s the rural population has been in continual decline. There were however odd periods and locations of expansion; for example, in some parts of the country, rural housing was provided for soldiers returning from the Great War. There were also the Bord na Mona schemes des-cribed above. On the other hand, the decline in population lifted the physical pressures off the countryside. The Land Acts gave the farmers ownership of their land and there was a general improvement in the appearance of the landscape. Land consolidation took place with replanting of hedgerows and trees around small fields.

1960s to the Present

Since the 1960s Ireland has experienced for the first time in a hundred years a significant rise in population. The rise is particularly noticeable in the cities and towns. Rural population has tended to stabilise, with growth in some parts and decline in others. Agricultural employment however continued to decline and the rural growths have involved the non-farm population. In the period 1956 to 1971 the population in the open countryside declined by 12.8 per cent, but from 1971 to 1981 increased by 7.4 per cent. (The census definition of rural population is the population in the open countryside, including clusters of fifty persons or under).

Recent statistics on house building in Ireland (An Foras Forbartha, 1984) show that the number of single houses has increased from 23% of the national total of all houses built in 1976 to 41% in 1983. In 1983, 96% of new single houses had private septic tank drainage. This would indicate that approaching 40% of all new houses built in the country are now outside the main urban areas, and indeed many smaller towns and villages. With regard to house types, in 1983, 78% of the new single houses were bungalows.

The implications for the rural landscape of this present trend could, over a period of years, be disastrous. The traditional rural population is declining, and is being replaced by a new type of "suburban community" whose aesthetic values are being imposed on the countryside. Paradoxically, the deterioration has occurred while a comprehensive system of physical planning was being established in the country. There is need for a new locational policy with regard to housing and also design controls in respect of housing, wherever it is built, but particularly when it is built in the open countryside.

PLANNING CONTEXT

The preamble to the 1963 Local Government (Planning and Development)
Act was "an Act to make provision in the interest of the common
good for the proper planning and development of cities, towns, and
other areas, including urban or rural (including the preservation
and improvement of the amenities thereof)". This Act remains the
foundation for the entire system of planning controls operated in
the country. One of the act's fundamental aims was the preservation of rural amenities. Although rural amenities were not specifically defined then (or in subsequent regulations) it was universally
accepted that the term included the lowland countryside and not
only areas of outstanding natural beauty such as the coastline,
mountains, and lakes. The planning policies formulated by most
County Councils confirm this view, and, in particular, reveal an
awareness that rural amenities can be affected by intensive new
housing in the countryside. The majority of county plans contain
provision to:

(a) Prohibit isolated new housing in the countryside and also
     along the national primary and secondary traffic routes.

(b) Direct all new housing into existing settlements.

The main reasons for such provisions were to achieve a more balanced social structure, to make more economic use of services, and to
preserve the rural landscape. These policies, well meaning in
themselves, were often however diluted by phrases such as "in as
far as possible" or "exceptions will be made if a farmer wishes to
build a house for himself or a relative". The principles were
further diluted by establishing specific guidelines for new

building in supposedly prohibited areas. As in many other cases
the exceptions became the rule, and a laudable concept of gathering
new housing into existing rural settlements did not materialise.
Long stretches of main and secondary roads have acquired a corridor
of suburban-type development. There was, of course, a need for new
houses; the country was prospering and the whole psychological and
tax system was, and is, geared towards private property ownership.
In many cases people were only one generation removed from the
land, there were few alternative locations actually provided and
the planning process was passive rather than directive.

Leahy (1984) has established that a significant proportion of
people now living in rural areas would have preferred to live in
towns and villages if sites were available at a reasonable cost.
The comparative cheapness, particularly to the individual, of
acquiring a rural site, as opposed to one in a village or town,
was often a determining factor. However, public costs, or the
long-term social implications, were rarely considered at this stage.
A generation of home-owners and family makers was lost to the
existing settlements where it could have made important social and
economic contributions.

A fundamental objective of planning is to improve the aesthetic quality of new building. However, this objective has never
really been taken seriously, either in rural or urban situations.
Many plans have quite detailed regulations regarding the siting of
filling stations, car parking standards, the widths of roads, and
other matters. In rural contexts there are often special criteria
for entrances to new buildings, but little reference to orientation,

landscaping, and respect for regional building techniques. In
recent years there have been some improvements in this regard,
and some county plans do draw attention to the importance of
siting and building materials. There is little evidence however
of any great improvement on the ground.

The same lack of concern for aesthetic and design matters
applies to villages and small towns. Very few specific plans have
been prepared which deal with the techniques involved in improving
village building or inserting new buildings into the existing
structure. Whenever small settlements are considered in detail,
more often than not the techniques and policies formulated are
similar to those in larger towns and cities.

The results of recent new building in small settlements have
been disappointing. It is quite common to see suburban-type houses
and bungalows fitted into a village street, with little respect for
the neighbouring buildings. Village pubs and shops are often
modernised, and, as a result, have more in common with city
situations using, for example, large plastic signs and shopfronts.
This contrasts with many parts of Europe where there are often
quite strict building and design controls in rural villages.

The essence of the problem is not a need for new legislation,
although the existing legislation could be tidied in some aspects,
but for positive use of the planning legislation which we now have.
Unfortunately this disregard for sensible laws and regulations is
a widespread feature of modern Irish society, prevailing in many
spheres as well as planning.

The major thrust for the rest of this paper is that the

current policy of allowing random house building in the countryside has serious implications for the aesthetic and landscape qualities of our traditional lowland countryside; that it adds significantly to public and private costs; and that the continued development in the countryside is at the expense of the smaller towns and villages.

IMPLICATIONS

Aesthetic/Landscape

Most new rural housing is in the farmed countryside, where traditionally all dwelling houses were related to farming in some form or other. However the design philosophy of these new houses is a suburban one. The most popular source is the books of standard house plans, which draw their main inspiration from suburban house types. Building plots are uniform - approximately 100 ft x 100 ft; the houses are located in a regimental fashion, directly facing the road and with a uniform building line as determined by planning conditions, and the attention to site planning and landscaping is no different than in the normal suburban situation. Frequently, the entire site is cleared of hedges, trees and other natural features before building commences. There appears to be a desire to create a suburban atmosphere, rather than adopt a distinctive design approach influenced by the landscape characteristics and local building techniques.

Entire districts are being changed through this process. Drive from Dublin to Trim, or from Athlone to Ballinasloe, and see how the impact of such developments can change what are essentially rural environments into continuous strips of development.

The building requirements of these quasi-rural households are rarely different from urban ones - they are in the country but not of it. The generally small size of building plots does not allow an opportunity to create a new private environment, which might derive inspiration from its rural setting. There is for example no space to keep animals or create vegetable gardens. Outbuildings, evolved from traditional layouts, would be useful and could create a more interesting visual setting for the entire group.

Economic/Social

The economic and social costs of new rural housing are of particular significance and deserve more serious studies. Generally the financial costs in acquiring a site in a rural situation are less than in an urban one. However, this net cost does not reflect the true cost of building in a rural situation. There are other costs involved for services, which every householder expects to have and which the community at large has to provide.

It has been estimated that the cost of providing capital services - electricity, telephone, public lighting, etc., in a dispersed rural situation, costs £4,800 per house, as opposed to £900 for a terraced house in a town (Leahy, 1984). The ongoing costs are also more expensive in relation to the rural house; approximately £80 per year for such matters as refuse collection, public street lighting, and school transport, as opposed to £16 per year for a terraced house in an urban situation.

There are also private costs - the additional costs of commuting for employment purposes; the absolute need for a second car for many rural households; the lack of choices with regard to

shopping, recreational facilities, schools; and lack of opportunities for teenagers. In recent times, security has become a problem.
Perhaps the safest place of all to live is in the centre of a small
village or town. Certainly to judge from reports in recent years
there are less crime problems here than in the larger cities and
open countryside.

Social/Community

The continued growth of housing in the countryside has meant that
many smaller towns and villages have not expanded in any significant way. Valuable opportunities to generate new community life in
the villages, where the social and economic influence of the new
households could be significant, have been lost. The Rural Housing
Organisation which started in County Clare, and has now spread to
other counties, is a welcome, but small exception to the general
trend, even though initially some of their schemes could have been
better integrated into the village structure. Traditionally, in
Ireland, the village was outward looking, providing a service for
the wider rural population; and was not as introspective as villages
in other European countries tended to be.

Irish villages, therefore, could take more housing. However,
those new houses which have been built in villages and small towns
are generally no more successful, in the architectural sense, than
their rural counterparts are. If there is to be a serious policy
of directing new houses into existing settlements this should go
hand in hand with a new approach to design and siting.

FUTURE POLICIES

We must now assume that our population will continue to increase:
present trends suggest that it will be approaching four million at
the end of the century. Whether population will continue to expand
at the same rate in the early part of the next century is debatable.
We do not yet know what effect on population the recent renewal of
emigration will have. The new emigrants are likely however to be
in the younger age bracket.

It can be safely assumed too that the demand for new houses
will continue, and that the social objective of each household
having a separate dwelling will remain. This is such a fundamental
aspect of society, it is hard to visualise a change in the for-
seeable future. Separate accommodation need not necessarily always
mean individual houses, but in most cases we must assume that it
will be so.

Another assumption is that the Planning Acts will continue in
some form or other, and, therefore, the control of building and
development will be exercised by the community in the interest of
the common good.

However, any policy to restrict new housing in the countryside
must go hand in hand with a policy to renew the centres of our towns
and cities. This is another major planning problem of our times,
which has yet to be tackled in a decisive manner. (Urban Renewal
in Ireland, P. Shaffrey, 1980). Can we devise therefore an
alternative strategy to the present which consists of paying lip
service to the development of existing settlements but in practice
adopting a quite liberal approach to ad hoc rural building?

Small Towns and Villages

There are approximately one thousand small settlements, ranging from a few houses grouped around a crossroads up to small towns of around five hundred population. Within and immediately adjacent to such settlements there is significant scope for an increase in population without causing great social or physical disruption. Many villages of say two hundred persons could, over a period of ten to fifteen years, increase their population by 50% in a gradual fashion by building on gap sites, rounding off existing development and intensifying existing uses. In the process the villages could be made more interesting and attractive; small hamlets could be transformed into more interesting groupings, with perhaps the new houses grouped around a new village green.

These small settlements are extremely well distributed throughout the countryside and provide the possibility of a truly rural and yet cohesive social life. Services of all kinds are more economically provided and, ultimately, there is a physical sense of community - something which tends to be overlooked, but which is, in the long term, quite important.

Every Local Authority should have a development policy in respect of their villages and hamlets, as well as the towns, stressing the advantages of village living, the neighbourliness, social cohesion, security and additional opportunities for older people and younger households. Incentives should be provided for village groups, perhaps by increasing development charges for rural building and decreasing them for villages or providing more housing sites for community groups and individuals. It is important that

there is an aesthetic policy for every village with a clear
recognition that each has its own distinctive quality deriving
from relationships with the surrounding landscape, the types of
buildings and open spaces.

Countryside

There must be a fresh approach to the complex question of rural
land use planning. The problems caused by the ad hoc approach of
recent decades will have to be tackled and effective policies devised for the future. There are a number of crucial aspects.

Areas already Suburbanised

These areas should be clearly identified in County Plans, and a
primary objective of future policies should be gradually to trans-
form them from a suburban type environment into one with distinctive visual characteristics. This means comprehensive landscaping
plans, implemented jointly by the Local Authority and the new
residents. This will involve tree planting and hedgerow building;
retention of, and provision of new stone walls and other local
features. Some new housing may be allowed, if only to round off
existing developments and to provide a more definite break between
new developments and the traditional rural landscape. In this
event very strict guidelines with regard to design and siting would
be required. There is a need for better standards in general tidiness and maintenance. It is disappointing to note how frequently
the gardens of many new rural houses remain in an unfinished state
for years.

Other Rural Areas

Rural districts where relatively little development has taken place

should also be clearly identified in the Plans and future policies
should aim to retain their essential characteristics. New urban
type housing must be restricted so that these areas of genuine
countryside may be protected for the next generation. There is
really little room for manoeuvre here, but if the areas are clearly
and sensibly defined in the Plan then the general body of public
opinion will respect the restrictions.

National Primary and Secondary Roads

No more development should be allowed with direct access on to
national, primary or secondary roads. There should be a specific
government directive on this point, and no exceptions should be
made even for adjacent landowners. Sites along a busy traffic
route are the last place for family housing, and particularly as,
in the future, there will be more and more traffic carrying a
variety of goods with a significant number toxic and highly explos-
ive. If a question of compensation arises then that should be
faced up to. It is hard to credit that today there is still any
debate about this matter, and that some County Councils are so
ambivalent on the point.

The building of new roads, and the improvement and maintenance
of existing ones, should be considered as a major landscape issue,
and not merely a traffic engineering one. There should be a
comprehensive policy for landscaping the national primary roads
throughout the country, perhaps on a county basis. In the future,
routes could be identified by the quality and type of the landscaping and roadside treatment - a policy long since taken for
granted in other European counties.

76

New Building

It is hardly to be expected that all rural building will cease, or that there will be a complete turnaround in existing policies. There is, therefore, a need for positive guidelines to ensure that new building, where it is allowed, conforms to certain design and landscaping criteria. Otherwise the entire rural landscape could eventually deteriorate.

First it must be recognised that it is a privilege for a person with an urban occupation to be allowed to build in rural areas. Those privileged must accept specific obligations, particularly of an aesthetic kind. All proposals for rural building should be accompanied by a landscaping plan to be implemented as a significant part of the project. This plan should take account of topography, planting, boundary features, and materials. No plan for building in rural areas should be accepted unless this landscaping policy is an integral part of it. There may be some mandatory requirements. For example, in hedgerow districts all boundaries should be hedges; and similarly in stone wall areas. The possibility of adopting a minimum plot size in rural areas should be considered, e.g. the early County Council standards of one acre. This would allow the creation of a localised environment with its specific rural characteristics. The guidelines should also deal with matters of siting, materials, design, etc. Ultimately however, it is not a question of preparing guidelines, but ensuring that their specific recommendations are adhered to. We have too many examples in the past of policy statements and documents which are ignored during the implementation process.

Specialist Skills

There should be a much more significant landscape input into all the plans and policies of rural County Councils. It is a poor reflection on our priorities that, at a time of growing emphasis on tourism, leisure and recreation, few, if any, rural County Councils retain the services of landscape consultants, and fewer again employ landscape professionals on a permanent basis. We cannot forever rely on the local garden centre and the personal interest of the Area Engineer.

CONCLUSION

Have we anything to learn from other countries or are they all wrong in preserving an acceptable aesthetic balance between town and countryside? Must we assume that our present schizophrenic approach is correct, i.e. supposedly tough policies in plans but a lax approach on day to day control?

There is now an immediate challenge which this generation must face up to. The fine aesthetic appearance of the rural land-scape is the outcome of social and economic activities over many generations. To retain it there should be a greater educational emphasis on countryside matters generally, on local building techniques, ecological issues, landscaping and planting. The aesthetic qualities of the rural landscape are equally as pleasing but much more vulnerable than the better known landscapes of mountains, coastlines, rivers, and lakes.

If this generation is not prepared to accept social and economic arguments for living in the smaller towns and villages, it should accept the aesthetic and landscape arguments. Otherwise the entire lowland countryside could, in a generation or two, become one vast suburb and future generations will not thank us for this situation. The alternatives suggested in this paper do not require massive financial investment, new training programmes or institutional change. In the final analysis they involve mostly common sense and a concern for things beautiful.

References

An Foras Forbartha, Private Housebuilding in Ireland, 1976-1983.

Leahy, M., Unpublished MRUP Thesis Alternatives to Town Generated Rural Housing, Dept. of Regional & Urban Planning, UCD, 1984.

Mitchell, Frank, The Irish Landscape, London, 1976, p. 208.

Shaffrey, Patrick & Maura, Irish Countryside Buildings, Dublin, 1985.

Shaffrey, Patrick, Urban Renewal in Ireland - An overview, Conference Proceedings, I.P.I., 1980.

FARMING AND THE LANDSCAPE

Richard Webb

INTRODUCTION

Farmland covers 83 per cent of our country, with 5 per cent woodland and about 0.05 per cent in nature reserves and national parks.
Farming is, therefore, the dominant land-use and it consequently
determines the landscape and wildlife of our countryside.

Traditional mixed farming, using few pesticides or fertilizers,
accommodated a wide variety of wildlife within a diverse landscape.
Since Ireland joined the Common Market, great changes have taken
place in Irish agriculture and farm productivity has increased.
Factors contributing to this increased productivity include
improved methods of grassland management, increased use of
fertilizers, more effective methods of weed control, improved
field drainage, the use of more powerful machinery requiring larger
fields and more intensive husbandry.   Farmers have responded well
to the call for increased productivity and have been backed by
research and advice and helped by a system of grant aid and price
supports.

THE PRESSURES

While such changes are necessary, they have sometimes been
accompanied by a decline in the diversity and visual quality of our
landscape with a consequent loss of wildlife habitats.   Hedges and
woods are often removed because they are considered to be redundant
to the needs of modern farming.   Other features of importance in
the landscape, such as heathland, wetlands, moorland and field
monuments are often lost through a failure to recognise their
significance.   Our historical heritage is particularly at risk,
with 30-40 per cent of archaeological features having been removed
from most counties and with up to 60 per cent being lost from the
Cork harbour area since 1940 (O'Kelly and Shee, 1976).   At this

rate of destruction the surviving monuments in that area could hardly be expected to survive to the end of the century. The problem is exacerbated through a lack of knowledge of effective low cost management methods which could be used to conserve such features.

While we may feel that such changes are of little consequence to us at the moment and that, for example, in some areas there may well be too many hedges for efficient farming, the increasing scale of the loss of landscape features and wildlife habitats which contribute to a diverse and ecologically balanced countryside, with no compensating improvements being made, is such that the quality of the countryside will decline. This will produce a landscape very different from that which the countryman and visitor alike values so highly today. Such a landscape will offer fewer natural resources for us to use and, in some cases, could lead to a decrease in production through the loss of shelter and other factors, quite apart from the destruction of our natural and cultural heritage.

In terms of the impact of agriculture on the landscape, Ireland comes off relatively well in comparison with our neighbours. For example, since 1945, Britain has lost 95 per cent of flower-rich permanent pastures, 80 per cent of lowland heaths, 60 per cent of chalk-downland and 50 per cent of ancient broadleaved woodlands. More damage has occurred in the last 40 years than in the preceding 400 years (Nature Conservancy Council, 1984).

In Ireland, because we have had no land-use surveys, we simply do not know what the situation may be. With the publication in 1981 by An Foras Forbartha of the book, 'Areas of Scientific Interest in Ireland', we were made aware of those areas important for wildlife, but we do not have the resources to monitor these sites and we know that many have since been damaged. Our greatest conservation problems seem to lie with water pollution, arterial drainage and the commercial exploitation of bogland, but two other features give cause for concern, namely woodlands and hedgerows.

DECIDUOUS WOODLANDS

Broadleaved, deciduous woodlands cover only 1.2 per cent of the
country, less if only high forest is concerned, yet such woods
account for 21 per cent of our areas of scientific interest.
Around 60 per cent of all existing broadleaved woodland was planted
before 1900 and is now approaching over-maturity and facing
increasing pressures for clearfelling and either reclamation to
agriculture or 'coniferization' (An Foras Forbartha, 1985).   Woods
around the country are also under pressure from fuelwood cutters,
such as the nationally-important St John's Wood in Roscommon, or
Loughlinstown Wood in County Dublin.   Faced with large, and
realistic, claims for compensation, local authorities are virtually
powerless to control the situation.   Although the amount of such
woodland in private hands is twice that in state ownership, the
private planting of broadleaved trees has virtually ceased, in spite
of generous grant-aid.   Only two acres (one hectare) was planted in
the whole country in 1980 (Forest and Wildlife Service pers. comm.).
Although it is not known how much woodland is being cleared at the
moment, because broadleaved woodlands are mostly overmature and are
unmanaged, the appearance of the countryside will change as such
woods are not being replaced.

HEDGEROWS

Hedgerows have considerable visual amenity in the countryside and
are extremely important as a wildlife habitat.   They are also
important for shelter and hedgerow trees have a potential timber and
fuel value in the local context.   Roadside hedgerow trees especially
have an effect on the landscape out of all proportion to their
numbers as they are seen by, and frame the views of, all who travel
through the countryside.   As they have relatively little influence
on agriculture they are more likely to be tolerated by farmers.

With the intensification of agriculture and the move to larger farm
machinery, there has been some pressure in recent years to remove
hedgerows and to enlarge fields.   Farm improvement grants include
assistance for the removel of hedgerows.   The increasing use of
mechanical hedge trimming may also be having an adverse effect on the
numbers of hedgerow trees.

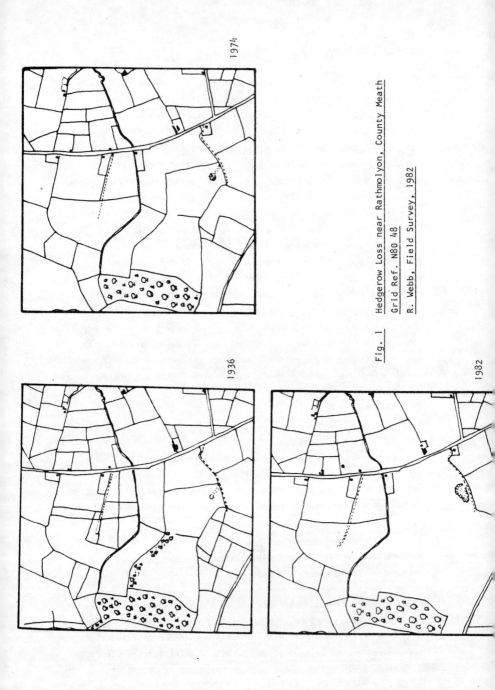

Fig. 1   Hedgerow Loss near Rathmolyon, County Meath

Grid Ref. N80 48

R. Webb, Field Survey, 1982

1936

1974

1982

In Britain there is increasing concern over the loss of hedgerows
and the fact that there are not enough young trees to replace those
dying of old age and Dutch elm disease.   In Ireland, however, the
state of the country's hedgerows is virtually unknown.

As part of An Foras Forbartha's report into the state of the
environment (An Foras Forbartha, 1985), a preliminary investigation
of hedgerow removal and of hedgerow trees has been carried out.
Over thirty randomly selected one-kilometre squares have been
examined around the country.   The length of hedgerows were measured
from the 1936 Ordnance Survey 6 inch scale maps, which were compared
with the 1973 air photographs available from the Geological Survey.
The present situation was then assessed in the field.   An example
of hedgerow loss in one km square in County Meath is illustrated in
Fig. 1.   Work will be continuing but preliminary results suggests
an average hedgerow loss of around 14 per cent since 1936, compared
with an average of around 30 per cent in Britain.   In some areas
there seems to have been a net gain in hedgerows due to land re-
organization.   Hedge removal appears to be localized, with more
removal taking place on the larger farms, irrespective of whether
they are tillage or grazing farms.   Areas of greatest clearance seem
to be in the south Laois - south Kildare area.

Nearly two-thirds of our bird species nest in hedges, and the
importance of hedgerows as a wildlife habitat can be seen when one
calculates the possible area of hedgerow habitat in the country.
Given that there is an average of 0.022 km² of hedge per km² and that
approximately 49,000 km² of land under crops and pasture may support
hedges, the total area of hedgerow habitat in Ireland may be in the
order of 1,078 km², or 1.5 per cent of the country.   This is three
times the area covered by deciduous high forest, or five times the
combined area of our four national parks.

HEDGEROW TREES

As there is virtually no information regarding the status of hedges
in Ireland, there is a corresponding dearth of information regarding
hedgerow trees.   In Britain, a Forestry Commission census in 1955

<u>Fig. 2</u> <u>Age Structure of Hedgerow Trees in Thirty One Kilometre</u>
<u>Squares</u>
<u>R. Webb, Field Survey 1984</u>

Species	Age Class				% of Total No.
	Sapling	Young	Mature	Overmature	
Ash	312	216	99	3	53%
Sycamore	10	63	25	1	8%
Beech	30	53	101	1	15%
Elm	40	38	42	6	10%
Oak	8	17	27	3	5%
Others (cherry, willow horse chestnut, rowan, holly, etc.)	41	36	12	1	7.6%
Total	441	423	306	15	1,185

estimated that hedgerow trees represented a fifth of the standing
timber at that time (HMSO, 1955), yet there has been a post-war
decline in the number of hedgerow trees in Britain of the order of
two per cent per annum, twice as high as the rate of hedgerow loss.
Those trees which remain are largely over-mature, and in many areas
there are not enough young trees to replace them.   It has been
calculated that six saplings are needed to replace one mature tree,
and that in much of lowland England this ratio is now around 0.4:1
(Countryside Commission, 1974).   It is not known how the status of
hedgerow trees in Ireland compares with these figures, whether there
is an appropriate distribution of age classes to ensure the continuity of the conservation and amenity value of hedgerow trees, and
if mechanised trimming is affecting the composition of hedges.

In order to obtain a possible guide to the status of hedgerow trees,
an examination of the trees in the thirty km squares was carried out.
A total of 1,185 trees were distributed among the four age classes of
'sapling', 'young', 'mature' and 'overmature', Fig. 2.   To ensure
replacement of trees and to allow for mortality, the numbers of
saplings should about equal the numbers of trees in all other classes.
As this is not the case in the survey areas (the situation being
broadly similar to England twenty years ago) (Forestry Commission,
1965), even if no more trees were felled, the total number will
decrease.   It is however difficult to assess the numbers of ash
saplings in tall hedges, so the ratio may be more favourable.   As
there are more saplings than semi-mature trees and both classes equal
the numbers of mature trees, the situation at first sight is not too
discouraging.

It is worth noting, however, the complete dominance of ash in all age
classes and the lack of saplings in all other species.   At 53 per
cent, ash forms a major hedgerow tree and saplings are vulnerable to
mechanical cutting.   It is not a very long-lived tree and being
shallow rooted is also vulnerable to cultivation.   In Britain, a
condition known as ash decline has been traced to the pressures of
cultivation.

Beech, while not a major hedgerow tree, was planted in vast numbers
during the last century as an amenity tree and for shelter.   It has

become an essential element in the Irish landscape, yet there are almost no saplings to replace the trees now dying of old age in increasing numbers. Over half of the trees damaged in last year's gales were over-mature beech. Oaks account for only 5 per cent of hedgerow trees and may be said to be uncommon in the countryside, outside of our native woods, a reflection of the degree of tree destruction in the early part of the 19th century.

Given the vulnerable nature of our hedgerow trees, the scenery of the lowland countryside is likely to change dramatically over the next twenty years unless extensive replanting is carried out. More detailed work on hedgerow analysis needs to be done at local level.

A FUTURE FOR THE LANDSCAPE

As farmland becomes managed more intensively there will be a greater need to manage parts of it more positively for nature conservation. 'Areas of Scientific Interest in Ireland' lists those areas which are important for conservation. Given the international importance of many of these areas, especially wetlands, conservationists are justified in asking the farming community not to reclaim the last remnants of good wildlife habitat that still exist.

In times when limits to farm production are being set in Brussels, the farmer still needs to maintain his income. He has the skills to manage a flower-rich hay meadow and if the public want a diverse landscape they should pay for it, or at least not pay for its destruction. A step in the right direction was made recently in Brussels where the agriculture ministers agreed to an alteration to the agricultural structures directive so that farmers could be assisted to carry on with traditional farming methods in ecologically sensitive areas.

RESPONSIBILITIES

Planning authorities, in effect, have little influence in the con-servation of landscape and wildlife except in certain well-defined

areas.   There are only 130 tree preservation orders in existence
and fourteen county councils have never made a TPO.   In practice
TPOs are unenforceable in the face of claims for compensation.   In
a similar fashion a potentially very useful tool for landscape
conservation and management, namely management agreements which can
be made under Section 38 of the Planning Acts, has never been used
because of the inability of the planning authority to pay a claim
for compensation.   Since 1963 only six special amenity area orders
have been drafted and none have been passed by the Minister for the
Environment.

The responsibility here rests with the Department of the Environment
in drafting clear guidelines for planning authorities on tree
preservation orders, management agreements and special amenity area
orders, and also in looking at the whole issue of compensation in
relation to these instruments.   The economic justification for doing
so lies in the fact that tourism, which earned us £808m in 1983, is
to a large extent based on Ireland having attractive landscapes for
visitors to enjoy.

Semi-state bodies and farm support organizations have also been lax
in their responsibilities to conservation.   Four years after the
publication of 'Areas of Scientific Interest in Ireland', the
Department of Agriculture can grant-aid the aerial spraying of the
Burren.   Fortunately the Forest and Wildlife Service has produced a
½" scale OS map showing the location of ASIs and these maps have been
circulated to local authorities but have not yet reached all the
local ACOT offices.

In the windiest country in Europe, ACOT can produce an advisory
leaflet on how to wallpaper your farmhouse but has nothing on how to
plant a shelter-belt.   Ireland must be unique in the EEC in having
no land-use survey, so that we do not know how the landscape is
changing in terms of the types, rates and areas of change.   As a
result we cannot monitor the effectiveness of our planning process.
The new high resolution satellite imagery obtainable from LANDSAT 5
may now enable a land-use survey to be carried out cheaply and
quickly.

The conservation of our wildlife habitats is also very unsatisfactory. Sixteen of the nineteen statutory nature reserves are woodland areas already owned by the Forest and Wildlife Service. Bogs and wetlands are very poorly protected in contrast with the national nature reserves in Northern Ireland.

The amount of money spend directly on wildlife conservation in Ireland, on research, publicity and education and the management of habitats, is derisory, a mere £171,763 in 1983, only 0.37 per cent of the budget of the Forest and Wildlife Service. This amounts to 5p per person in Ireland, the price of a box of matches. One may compare this figure with the £4,680,000 expenditure on the arts, by the Arts Council, which works out at £1.33 per person, the price of a pint of Guinness.

The conservation movement in Ireland is very small and fragmented and, unlike the farmers, has not generated any kind of political lobby with which to put forward their views. They still talk in aesthetic terms, instead of speaking the same language as the farmer in terms of economics or land management. They are unable to make hard economic justifications for their cases and even lack fundamental data, although new research from the Game Conservancy is changing this.

Farmers should continue to take advantage of developments aimed at increasing the efficiency of the agricultural industry. At the same time it is essential that such developments do not cause needless harm to our landscape and wildlife heritage, itself the basic resource of our tourism industry. Successful commercial farming can be integrated with conservation if farmers take stock of the landscape and wildlife features on the farm, plan ahead so that future development of the farm takes account of its appearance and wildlife and take positive action to manage the farm operations sympathetically and to establish features which may have been lost from the farm.   '

Farmers may say, 'but conservation costs money and time I can ill afford'. In most cases, however, all that is needed is a change in the methods of farm management. Farmers could actually benefit from conservation in several ways including:

Increasing Revenue

- Improving sporting or timber values.

- Increasing shelter with hedgerows and shelterbelts. In some cases shelterbelts can improve livestock yields by up to 20 per cent.

- Providing fuel wood or timber for use on the farm.

- Retaining an attractive and interesting landscape so as to benefit from farm-based tourism.

Improving Cost-Effectiveness

- Maintaining a diversity of wildlife habitats to ensure a healthy ecological balance, so that insects can pollinate crops and predators keep pest species under control.

Making Farm Management Easier

- Providing shelterbelts and hedges.

Maintaining a Pleasant Environment for the Farmer and his Family, and for the Community

- Enhancing the landscape with features that facilitate country pursuits.

We sometimes hear that farmers are not interested in conservation and that they see it as being incompatible with modern farming, a view which is encouraged by the farming press. There is also a widespread and negative view that farmers are not to blame for water pollution or habitat destruction and that much more damage is done by local authorities and industry. As we have seen, however, the conservation of soil, water and wildlife is necessary for agricultural production. Recent surveys in Britain have shown that many farmers are interested in environmental conservation even though they may be hostile to conservationists! Many farmers also expressed a desire to improve the appearance and interest of their

89

living and working environment, provided that this would not entail
significant interference with farming operations and profit levels.
More often than not, farmers also demonstrated a genuine interest in
finding out what valuable features existed on their farms and how
they could best be conserved at the lowest cost.   Many farmers, of
course, particularly those with an interest in field sports, are
already demonstrating that good farming and conservation do co-exist.

In order to help farmers with practical advice on aspects of countryside conservation and management, a series of advisory leaflets has
been prepared by An Foras Forbartha and a booklet on Farming and
Wildlife is available free from the Forest and Wildlife Service.
Conflicts of interests may occur, but in most cases they can be
resolved by understanding and negotiation.   In an effort to achieve
this, An Taisce has formed the Farming and Conservation Liaison
Group with the main farming and farm support groups and conservation
bodies, to act as a national forum for the discussion of farming and
conservation issues.

CONCLUSION

In conclusion we can define conservation as the wise use of land and
other resources available to the farmer.   It embraces food production,
forestry, sporting activities, rural recreation and education, soil
conservation, the protection, provision and management of wildlife
habitats, the preservation of historic features and the visual
enhancement of the landscape.   Such a definition leads to the idea
that the management of land for uses in addition to food production
could be feasible on commercial farms.   In Britain, this idea is
being tested by the Demonstration Farms Project, run by the Countryside Commission, which is assessing the practical opportunities
which exist on commercial farms for changing management practices in
the interests of improving visual, historic and wildlife features,
whilst still maintaining farm profits (Countryside Commission, 1984).

The rural landscape which we currently enjoy is a legacy inherited
from those who planted the landscape and managed it in a certain way.

Many landscape features are now deteriorating and are not being replaced. The problem is appreciated by the general public, for in 1983 an EEC survey found that the major environmental concern of Irish people was the deterioration of the landscape.

The halt in the deterioration of our landscape can only be reversed if a package of improvement measures is planned and implemented. Such a package would include policies, incentives, advice and controls, including:

1. At EEC level, a revision to the Agricultural Structures Directive to accommodate conservation as a legitimate land-use alongside agriculture, and financial assistance for conservation measures.

2. Revisions in legislation to overcome the problems of compensation.

3. Guidelines from the Department of the Environment to planning authorities as to how to use the statutory conservation instruments.

4. From the state bodies, a modified set of supports for the rural community based on a reallocation of existing resources.

5. A nationwide land-use survey based on a partnership of agricultural support organizations and universities.

6. Advice on the management of landscape features such as deciduous woodlands and wetlands and a more balanced consideration of conservation objectives from all advisory and extension services.

7. From farmers and landowners, the preparation of farm plans which take conservation into account in response to positive incentives.

8. From the media, promoting the benefits to be gained from rural landscape conservation and management.

Because the landscape has always resulted from a response to economic policies, the single most important measure would be the creation of a

commercial climate in which farmers are positively encouraged to use
and manage their land in the joint interests of production and
conservation.

References

An Foras Forbartha, Areas of Scientific Interest in Ireland, Dublin,
                    1981.
An Foras Forbartha, The State of the Environment, Dublin, 1985.
Countryside Commission, New Agricultural Landscapes, CCP76,
                    Cheltenham, 1974.
Countryside Commission, Agricultural Landscapes; Demonstration Farms,
                    CCP170, Cheltenham, 1984.
Forest and Wildlife Service, Farming and Wildlife, Dublin, 1985.
Forestry Commission, Census of Woodlands, HMSO, London, 1965.
Merthyr Committee, Report of the Committee on Hedgerow and Farm
                    Timber, HMSO, London, 1955.
Nature Conservancy Council, Nature Conservation in Great Britain,
                    London, 1984.
Nature Conservancy Council, Nature Conservation and Agriculture,
                    London, 1977.
O'Kelly and Shee, E., Memorandum on the Archaeology of Cork Harbour,
                    Cork, UCC, Cork, 1976.

FORESTS IN THE LANDSCAPE

Gregory Dunstan

INTRODUCTION : THE FOREST ESTATE IN IRELAND

The Forest Estate and its Management

In 1979 there were 328,500 hectares (811,700 acres) of forests
in Ireland, excluding areas felled, areas of scrub, and areas
unplanted. This represents 4.8% of the land area of the
Republic. 85% of this area was owned by the State in forests
managed by the Forest and Wildlife Service (F.W.S.). Of the
state forests (280,600 ha.), 94% of their area was under coniferous
trees. 68% of the coniferous forest was twenty years old and
under, and 88% thirty years old and under.   In contrast with
the State plantations, only 32% of private forests were
coniferous and only 49% of those were aged 30 years and less. 44%
of all private forest area was under broadleaf trees aged 71 years
and more (Forest and Wildlife Service, 1980/83, p.43) (Figures 1
and 2). In assessing the visual impact of forests, especially in
comparison with long-established (and often well-loved) broadleafed
woodlands, it is important to bear in mind their youth. The average
rotation length of coniferous forests in Ireland (on sylvicultural
rather than economic criteria) is approximately 50 years. Two
thirds of the State coniferous plantations would not have reached
the age of their first thinning by 1979.

Except for the hazards of damage to plantations by wind, Ireland
has the most favourable climate for timber production in Europe.
Forestry yields are expressed in terms of the mean volume of timber
produced per hectare per year, over the length of the rotation.

FIGURE 1 : STATE PLANTING FROM 1920 TO 1980.

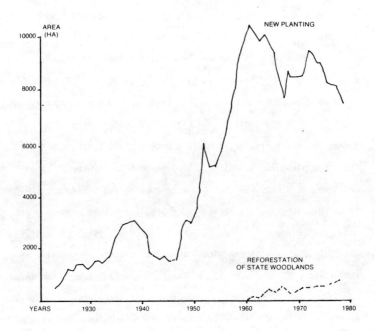

Source : Forest and Wildlife Service, 1980/83, p.5.

FIGURE 2 : AGE CLASS DISTRIBUTION OF FORESTS 1979.

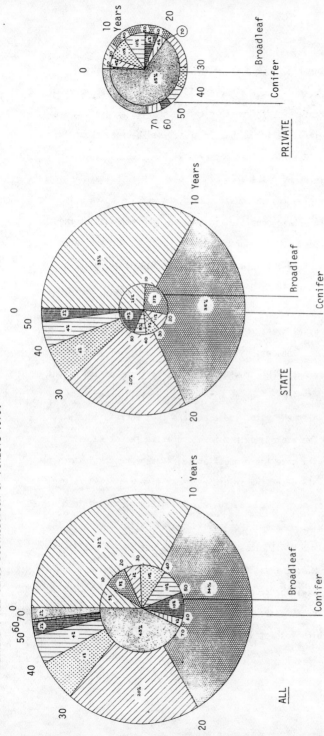

Notes: 1. Excludes scrub, felled and undeveloped areas.
        2. State broadleaf woodland over 50 years old includes older categories also.

Source : Forest and Wildlife Service, 1980/83, p.43.

The resulting figure (e.g. 13 m^3/ha./yr.) can be expressed
as a Yield Class (i.e. Yield Class 13). Including estimates
for the large areas of forest which are not yet producing even
thinnings, it is believed that Irish forests average about
Yield Class 13 to 14. This compares with estimated average
European yields of class 2 to 5, and class 10 in Britain, in spite
of a restriction to poor quality land, as will be noted below.
In spite of certain penalties in terms of the strength of the
timber produced, the favourable growth rate, and an estimated
real return of 3%-5%, establish a case in favour of coniferous
forestry as a valid land use in Ireland.

The length of a forest rotation, the time from planting to
harvesting, is conventionally defined as the age of maximum mean
annual increment. The growth of a tree, in terms of its height
and volume of timber, varies with time, initially slow,
accelerating in early to middle age and then decreasing towards
maturity. The age of maximum mean annual increment (M.A.I.) is the
age which will give the highest annual average growth in the volume
of timber. In practice, in order to maximise financial return,
the rotation may be reduced to less than that of the maximum M.A.I.
Current F.W.S. management policy is to fell Sitka Spruce at the
age of maximum M.A.I. less 20%, Norway Spruce and Lodgepole Pine
at maximum M.A.I. less 30% (Forest and Wildlife Service, 1980/83,
p.23). A Sitka Spruce of Yield Class 24 (very rapid growth) felled
at 50, 40 and 80 years of age would be approximately 33, 28 and
40 metres high respectively.

Rotation length has an important bearing on the landscape of
forests. First, forest rotations may be contrasted with the
annual crop cycles of tillage farming. Although of relatively
limited seasonal change, a coniferous forest landscape is
not static, but develops over a cycle of perhaps 40 to 50 years.
During this time the trees become established, the canopy closes
and becomes a thicket, thinnings are undertaken and the crop
is finally felled. Second, even at the age of maximum M.A.I.,
trees have not reached the height and girth which they might obtain
if left to grow to natural maturity. This effect is more pronounced
if the rotation length is reduced. Again, the difficulty is pointed
up of comparing even "mature" plantations with long established
broadleaf woodland, often containing trees of much greater age.
Coniferous plantations and old broadleaf woods have been developed
by very different management processes, and their landscapes should
not be compared without bearing this difference in mind.

Irish state forests are widely distributed over the country.
The largest areas are in the upland and mountain areas of Wicklow,
the Slieve Bloom, Slieve Aughty, the mountains of south and south
west Munster, and in Galway/Mayo (Figure 3). Early planting was
concentrated mainly in the south east. However, following
technical advances in ploughs and heavy tractors, the principle
expansion of planting since the fifties took place in Munster and
Connaught (Figure 4). In 1981 Cork, Galway and Mayo were the first
three counties in terms of forest land. In the same year Mayo
and Galway saw the highest and second highest areas of State planting,
and were the highest and (after Cork, Kerry and Donegal) fifth highest
in terms of plantable area acquired. In 1982 Galway and Mayo held

STATE FORESTS

1:1250.000

FIGURE 3 : LAND OWNED BY STATE FOREST AUTHORITIES 1972.

Source : Royal Irish Academy, 1979, p.65.

38.6% of all F.W.S. plantable reserve. A map of private forests
would show small areas widely dispersed, and lacking the relative
concentrations of state planting in some upland areas.

Two points should be noted about the location of state forests:
their fragmentation, and their restriction to areas of poor quality
soil. The Minister of Fisheries and Forests has powers of
compulsory purchase. These are seldom used, except to facilitate
the equable division of commonage, and most land has been acquired
on foot of offers by owners. Whatever the difficulties for
efficient layout and management of forests under these circumstances,
the operation of such a system of acquisition severely restricts the
opportunities for considering the visual effects of forest siting.
The restriction to areas of poor quality land has been enforced
to avoid competition with agriculture. In 1926 the Minister for
Agriculture stated "The Department do not desire to acquire for
afforestation land fit for agricultural purposes which might be
capable of being used to form new holdings or to enlarge existing ones.
With a view, therefore, to preventing such land from being acquired
for afforestation, they have fixed a maximum price at such a figure
as to render its sale to the Department for this purpose an uneconomic
transaction" (quoted in Farrell, 1983, p.157). With periodic
revisions of the permitted price, this system, in essence, has
continued to operate up to the present.

A consequence of this control on land acquisition has been that,
except for some old demesnes, most afforestation has taken place
on "bare land", mostly, again, in upland or mountainous regions,
and often in scenic areas. In such areas landform is usually the
dominant physical factor in the appearance of the landscape.

Its form, and the vegetation patterns on it, reflect the operation of natural processes, past and present. There is seldom a framework of man-made features such as hedgerows and small woodlands which would provide a visual context for afforestation. Relative height, and steep slopes add to the visual exposure of these areas. Their afforestation, therefore, will often result in significant visual impact. A reliance on the land market, precluding planning of acquisition in both space and time, does not help.

The quality of land afforested, the requirements of the timber market and the commercial requirement for relatively short rotations affect the choice of species used. Before 1945, the principal conifers used were Scots Pine and Norway Spruce. The bulk of the expansion of planting since then has been achieved with Sitka Spruce and Lodgepole Pine (Figure 5). Sitka Spruce will give similar yields to Norway Spruce, but on poorer soils. Lodgepole Pine will grow on deep peats and very poor mineral soils (e.g. on some Old Red Sandstone sites) and in conditions of severe exposure where Spruce will not thrive. The distribution and mean yield classes of the principal species used in the Republic are set out in Table 1.

TABLE I - SPECIES DISTRIBUTION AND YIELD CLASS

Species	% Distribution		Yield Class
	State	Private	
Sitka Spruce	44	9	15
Lodgepole Pine	26	-	11
Scots Pine	6	7	8
Norway Spruce	9	5	16
Larches	4	5	8
Other Conifers (incl. mixtures)	6	5	-
Oak	1.2	17	-
Beech	1.6	16	-
Ash	0.5	11	-
Other Broadleaves	1.7	25	-

Source : O'Carroll, 1984, pp.36-7.

TABLE II - AREAS FOR CLEARFELLING, 1985-2014

Period	Mean Annual Area Felled (Ha.)
1985-1989	1688
1990-1994	1703
1995-1999	2875
2000-2004	5373
2005-2009	7210
2010-2014	7491

Source : Forest and Wildlife Service, 1980/83, p.58.

Current Developments

There is evidence of several changes in the pattern of forestry
as it has developed over the last thirty years:-

- An increasing annual area of clearfelling as the
  old plantations reach the end of their first
  rotation.
- An apparent willingness to consider "marginal"
  agricultural land for afforestation, instead of land
  unsuitable for agriculture.
- A relative concentration by the F.W.S. on land in
  prime acquisition areas, with, for the present, a
  reduced annual planting target.
- The beginnings of significant private sector
  afforestation, partly funded by pension funds and
  other institutional investors, and partly undertaken
  by individual landowners.

Significant clearfelling and restocking starting in the early 1960's,
and reached 1,000 ha. per annum or more in the early 1980's.
Given the principle of sustained yield by which forest management
is governed, areas for clearfelling up to AD 2015 are not influenced
by policy changes, and can be predicted. Five-year mean areas for
clearfelling of State forests are shown in Table II.   Short
of some unforeseen circumstance, a rapid acceleration of clearfelling
may be expected in the mid-1990's. Where it occurs, clearfelling
produces a much more immediate change in the landscape than initial
planting.

Instead of concentrating on land unsuitable for forestry, an
emphasis on the afforestation of "marginal" land can be
detected:-

> "There is a growing general acceptance that much
> of the land classified as marginal for agriculture
> (representing 40% of the land of the country) could
> profitably be devoted to forest crops" (Paddy
> O'Toole, T.D., 23:11:1984).
> "39,000 acres, mainly in the West, are to be
> afforested with IR£14 million of E.I.B. (European
> Investment Bank) loans. The land involved is
> considered marginal for agriculture" (R.T.E. Radio
> News, 10.00 p.m., 14:1:1985).

"Marginality" of land is an economic concept, referring to its
ability or inability to yield a return to a given enterprise.
49.6% of Ireland is occupied by land classified as marginal for
agriculture, due to wetness, shallow soils, steep slopes, organic
soils, rockiness, or adverse climate. 21% of this marginal land
is classified as highly productive to forestry, and occurs mainly
on wet mineral lowland soils. The balance would be classified as
marginal for both forestry and agriculture (Bulfin, 1984).

It should be noted that what is involved here is a change of
emphasis, related to developments in the agricultural economy of
Ireland and of Western Europe. As agriculture generally intensifies,
the point (in terms of productivity and income thereby generated) at
which agricultural land becomes marginal rises. The effect of this

emphasis on marginal land (both on the areas most productive for forestry, and also on others) may be to permit afforestation in areas where it has not been much practised so far (the drumlin belt of Leitrim to Monaghan, parts of Clare, north Kerry and west Limerick, and the Castlecomer plateau of Co. Kilkenny). It may also permit forestry on the lower slopes of some mountain and upland areas, with less pressure on the higher slopes. The effects on the landscape of the Drumlin belt in particular will be considered later. The effects on the landscape of upland areas may be generally beneficial, provided that the mountains do not become "divorced" from surrounding lowlands by extensive belts of forest.

From about 1980 onwards, acquisition policy in the F.W.S. has concentrated on consolidation of existing forest areas. Prime acquisition areas have been defined, although not announced. Such a policy has obvious attractions from the point of view of forest management, allowing economies in roading and rationalization of fences. The implications of this policy, and its implementation, for the landscape must vary from site to site. Where, by infilling between existing plantations, it may lead to the coalescence of relatively small blocks on hillsides, it may be welcome. If it leads to a dominance by forests of upland landscapes, with reduced contrast of open land, its effect may be negative. The issues of the scale of forests and their relation to topography are discussed below.

The Government's decision on the report subsequently published as The Case for Forestry (Forest and Wildlife Service, 1980/83) was:-

(a)   "that the annual national planting target of 10,000
        hectares should be maintained as an overall policy
        objective,

(b)   that, for the purpose of achieving this objective,
        reforestation and planting of privately owned land should
        be taken into account, and

(c)   that, pending an improvement in the land reserve
        situation in relation to State-owned lands and an
        acceleration of private forestry, an annual State
        planting programme, including reforestation, of the
        order of 7,500 hectares - to be augmented as much as
        possible by private planting - should be accepted as
        the most practical short-term policy for the next five
        years".

The target of 7,500 hectares annually for 1985-87 was confirmed in
the document Building on Reality (1984), albeit in less precise
terms. This level of planting was first achieved and surpassed in
the later 1950's. Should the present interim policy be continued,
land acquisition for State planting would effectively cease in about
thirty years time (Forest and Wildlife Service, 1980/83, p.28).
At this point the area being felled would approximately balance the
planting target (compare Table II). The area of State forest would
then be approximately 440,000 hectares, or $6\frac{1}{4}$% of the Republic's
area. However, such a prognosis is hedged with conditions and un-
certainties:

The private forest sector is remarkably small by European
standards. However, there is evidence that it is beginning
to grow. The first pension fund investment in forestry was undertaken in 1981, when Allied Irish Investment Bank bought two
plantations totalling 90 hectares in Co. Clare, on behalf of a
pension fund. Cash flow profiles of well-managed forests, with
their relatively long timescale to clearfelling are well matched
to the liabilities of pension funds. It has been estimated that
IR£5-10 million could be available from this source for forestry
investment (O'Loughlin, 1984). In contrast to this
institutional interest, there has been rather little planting
by private landowners. Uptake of grants of 85% of approved costs
for farmers, 70% of approved costs for others, available under the
E.E.C.-financed "Western Package" from 15th April 1981 has so far
reached only 10% (The Irish Times, 23:2:1985). (Some of these
grants will have gone to institutional investors). The reasons
probably lie in the long period between investment and the
generation of an income from forestry, social factors of unfamiliarity
with trees and a reported perception that to grow trees is a symbol
of failure as a farmer. It is not intended here to summarize an
already extension literature on the subject (e.g. Convery, 1979;
Convery and Dripchak, 1983; Farrell, 1983). It appears at present
that institutional investors are likely to lead, if they do not
dominate, the private sector industry. (67% of farmers interested
in energy crops or tree growing surveyed in the border area stated
a preference to rent their land, 23% to sell for energy crops, and
only 9% to grow their own energy crops (Convery and Dripchak, 1983,
pp.5, 103, 105). Land is available for purchase for investment

forestry, and the virtual abolition of the Land Commission has assisted this (Hussey, pers. comm., 1985). The rate and extent of private sector forest development, therefore, depends on the balance of a series of factors including the area and quality of land becoming available, land prices, the levels of grant aid for forestry and of support for agriculture, the taxation regime for forestry, and the expectations of the market for forest products.

The Forests : Conclusion

From this very brief review of some aspects of forests and forestry as practised in Ireland, some initial conclusions can be drawn:-

1. It is essential to recognise the constraints under which afforestation has been carried out when reviewing its impact on the landscape.

2. It is essential to have some understanding of forestry as a production system, with technical requirements and economic constraints. These both determine its impact in the landscape and affect the design and management measures which may realistically be proposed to alleviate adverse impacts. Departures from normal practice affect the cost of, and return from, forestry operations.

3. Even under Irish conditions of growth, forestry has a long time-scale: one rotation in, perhaps $^{2}/3$ of a human lifetime. What has already been done can, in most cases, be altered very little (if at all) until the end of the present rotation at the earliest. Suggestions for remedial measures, therefore, are relevant to new plantations, and, in the longer term, to the second rotations of the existing forest estate.

THE VISUAL IMPACT OF FORESTRY

Some Definitions

Visual impact is a function of the characteristics of the
object having that impact, in relation to those of its
surroundings, and of distance from where it is observed. The
characteristics of the object could include its scale, shape,
height, colour, textures and patterns. Where the object is
complex, the arrangement of its components is important. All
these must be considered in relation to its surroundings, the
relationship (if any) between its characteristics and those of
its surroundings, and the effects of intervening features which
may screen it. The landscape is least changed where the impact
is "low" in quantity. It character is most changed by a "high"
impact, and its quality by the extremes of negative or positive
impact.

Some of the characteristics of coniferous forests make for
relatively high visual impact. The scale of afforestation tends
to be large, larger than traditional field sizes, and larger
than the fairly subtle patterns of vegetation change on open
upland hillsides. Shapes determined by acquisition lines defined
by surveyors and in legal documents may be uncompromisingly
geometrical, and obtrusive if no corresponding geometry exists
in the wider landscape. As forests develop, they begin to
appear as a mass, a "solid" contrasting with the openness of
bare hills or the "voids" of enclosed fields. They also enclose,
progressively obscuring areas beyond them. The textures of
coniferous trees, determined by their foliage and branch structure,
are usually coarser than those in their surroundings, so that

the forest appears as a dark element in the view. Their
evergreen character (larch excepted) contrasts with deciduous
trees and shrubs, and with the die-back of upland grasses
and bracken in autumn and winter. The characteristic blue-
green of Sitka Spruce and Scots Pine differs from the yellow-
greens more common in the traditional Irish landscape.

Afforestation, then, alters the character of a landscape. A
sequence of changes in this character can be envisaged:-

> Existing rural landscapes
>
> Forested rural landscapes (agriculture/open
> land visually dominant)
>
> Forest with farmland (forest visually dominant)
>
> Forest landscape

It is dangerous to divide a continuum of changing character into
categories, the more so as landscapes can be experienced at different
scales (e.g. the Westport drumlins as seen from among them, and
from Croagh Patrick), and are very seldom discrete, strongly bounded
units. What is important to note is that a change of character
runs ahead of the actual proportion of the area afforested. An
area will be perceived by most people travelling through it to be
completed afforested before it is. This is because of the "solid"
character of forests, and their effect in blocking longer views.
In any given area, the speed at which character changes will
depend upon factors of the existing landscape, especially topography,
and on the pattern in which afforestation develops. In certain
circumstances (e.g. a small-scale drumlin landscape) forestry might
become visually dominant before 50% of the area is afforested.

FACTORS OF INITIAL LAYOUT

Position

The visual impact of a forest is affected by its position in
relation to the following factors:-

- Principal roads and viewpoints.
- Local and regional topography.
- Water, as rivers and lakes.
- Local vegetation patterns, particularly
  hedgerows and woods.

These issues are interrelated. They can, perhaps, be best illustrated
by an example. The area around Lough Inagh and Derryclare Lough,
Co. Galway, has been quite extensively afforested. The area is
visible from the Recess-Kylemore road. Small areas of planting
lie between the road and Lough Inagh, and a rather larger area in
the foreground to Derryclare Lough, obscuring it. The bulk of the
planting is to the west of the lakes, on the lower slopes of Bencorr.
Here, as a background to the lakes, (which, as water does, attract
the eye) and on the relatively gentle footslopes, the forests
seem an appropriate element of the landscape. The foreground position
of the planting between the lake and road has a much greater visual
impact, and is, on balance, regrettable. It should also be noted
that the south-eastern part of Derryclare Wood, extending out
over the subtly undulating landscape characteristic of south
Connemara "reads" as a strong rather even line in conflict with
the topography.

III

Scale

Irish rural landscapes vary greatly in scale, from the small
scale of the drumlin belts to the broad scales of the Wicklow
mountains or the peatlands of North Mayo. Scale, as a factor
in the appearance of forests, is concerned with the proportion
of forests to open land, both within an area such as a valley
or group of valleys, and on an individual unit of topography,
such as a hillside. Scale is important not only in the view
from a point, but also in the experience of a traveller walking
or driving through forests. In the case of a general proportion
of open land to forest, open land provides contrast or even, if
there is enough of it, a setting.

In the Slieve Bloom, the open moorland on the high plateau provides
an important contrast to the forests of Glendelour, Glenregan
and Glendine West. Without this, the landscape would be one of
forest only, and would be visually the poorer. Particularly in
Glendelour, afforestation, judged on visual criteria, has already
gone too high. In North Mayo the very large forest between
Nephin Beg and Birreencorragh, at the head of Lough Feeagh, is
beginning to dominate the mountain landscape because of its scale,
and its extension from low ridges and valleys up the sides of the
mountains. Because of this the apparent height of the mountains is
diminished: the scale of the forest is beginning to override that
of the topography. After a detailed study of forestry in Glendalough
and its immediate environs, Meagher (1981) concluded that "no
further afforestation should take place in the study area". Again,
the loss of contrasting open land, and a damaging change in the
character of an important landscape were the reasons for this
recommendation.

Shape

The effect of shape on the visual impact of a plantation is
related to its scale. Small blocks of forest on a steep hillside are often out of scale with the larger topography. A geometrical
shape accentuates their intrusion, but unrelated scale is
usually the primary problem. Such small blocks may be seen,
for example, in Glenmalure, Co. Wicklow, and at Meenaglough, on
the south slope of the Ox Mountains, Co. Sligo, north east of Lough
Talt.

The shape, or outline of a plantation is determined by that of
the area acquired, less any area deemed unplantable because of rock
outcrops, drainage or elevation. The effect of its shape on a
forest's visual impact is related primarily to topography, and to
the elevation of a viewpoint relative to the forest. As slope
gradient increases, the overall outline of a forest on it
becomes more widely and easily seen. In lowland, agricultural
areas the forest outline will usually relate to existing hedgerows.
A shape consisting of straight lines is easily accepted, although
an indented outline is preferable to one of very long straight
lines (forests on Paddock Hill, Annamoe, and on the east slope
of Djouce Mountain, Co. Wicklow, for example). Similarly, in
lowland bogs, straight edges, again preferably indented, are
usually both acceptable and the obvious way to proceed for lack
of strong determining features.

On open hillside sites, apart from the general relationship with
gradient, outline is important in relation to skylines, to the form
of the topography on plan, and to changes in topography (e.g. from

hillside to valley floor). It should be noted that a skyline, seen from a valley floor or principal viewpoint, often does not coincide with the topographic crest. Probably the least desirable relationship of forest to skyline is where it and the forest edge coincide. From the open side, the line of trees, appearing relatively dark and with a serrated top line, can appear severely intrusive. A bad example can be seen on the west side of Glenletter, in the Slieve Bloom. It is preferable that that forest should extend right over the skyline (where this is low enough), or stop well short of it. In the latter case, the topography, and open land which reveals it, can be seen to encompass the forest and so contain it. Topography, having been moulded by ice, frost, and running water, generally has a flowing, plastic form. A geometric outline may conflict with this. Topography also has a characteristic "grain", related to the lines of flow of the elements which formed it (if not, also to the underlying rock strata). The mountain-and-valley landscapes of the south-west, and the alignments of drumlins, are the most obvious examples of this "grain". A mountain valley also has a characteristic "flow", up and down its length. Afforest-ation is best adapted to this "grain" and "flow". If both sides of a valley are afforested, and any flatter floor (where present), the apparent vertical range of the topography is reduced. (Some Slieve Bloom glens illustrate this point well). Forestry in the head of a steep valley, including slopes to both sides, may also break the "flow" of the valley by visually closing it. In visual terms, therefore, it is preferable to afforest either one side of a valley only, or both sides leaving the valley bottom in agricultural/pastoral use (if this can be justified), or at least so to design the internal and species layout of the forest itself that it reflects the underlying landform.

The detailed treatment of forest edges will be reviewed below.
The following general guidance for the forest outline in
relation to topography can be given:-

- Relate edges (and therefore acquisition
  boundaries) to features of the landscape
  (streams, rock outcrops, spurs, existing scrub
  or woodland) wherever possible. (A good
  example may be seen east of the Owenaher River,
  south of Masshill, in the Ox Mountains, Co.
  Sligo).

- Avoid long, straight, vertical lines on bare
  hillsides: flowing, or short straight, roughly diagonal
  lines are usually preferable.

- The top edge should not follow a contour:
  this "reads" as a straight, horizontal line
  from a distance. It is preferable to bring
  the edge down over spurs (where climatic
  exposure is likely to be greater, in any case),
  and to push it up small side-valleys and re-
  entrants. The forest at Lough Inagh, on the footslopes of Bencorr, would benefit from such
  treatment. This approach has been developed by
  forester-landscape architects working within
  the British Forestry Commission, and would seem
  to be applicable in Ireland (Lucas, 1983; Campbell, 1977).

FIGURE 4 : TREND IN FOREST PLANTING BY PROVINCE (Smoothed data).

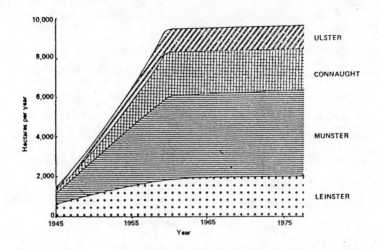

Source : Industrial Development Authority, 1981, p.47.

FIGURE 5 : TREND IN FOREST PLANTING BY SPECIES (Smoothed data).

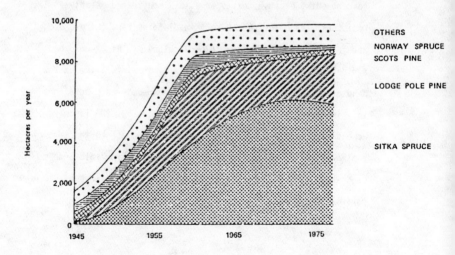

Source : Industrial Development Authority, 1981, p.48.

Colour and Texture

The characteristic colour and texture of coniferous trees,
and their contrast with more traditional landscape features,
was referred to above. For reasons of management, foresters
generally prefer stands of single species to mixtures. The use
of "nurses" of short term species (e.g. Japanese larch or
Lodgepole pine for Sitka Spruce), to be cut out early in the
rotation, is an exception. Intimate mixing of species may
present problems of forest management if their growth rates differ.
For this reason, the species layout of a forest is generally best
considered, in visual terms, as an arrangement of masses of
varying colour and texture. The boundaries between different
species (which will be selected on sylvicultural grounds) should be
related to features of the site as far as possible. Geometric
divisions should be avoided. It has been the practice to plant
bands of larch around the edges of forests, and sometimes between
compartments, because this species was considered relatively fire-
resistant. Examples can be seen in Glendine East (Slieve Bloom)
and in Glendasan/Glendalough (Co. Wicklow). This should be
avoided wherever possible: particularly in winter, the narrow
band of deciduous larch highlights the edge of the plantation: if
this is already unsympathetic to the topography, the larch
accentuates it. If species must be changed close to the edge of
a plantation (for relative fire-resistance, or for tolerance to
exposure), the edge species should be planted as a mass of
sufficient and variable depth not to "read" as a line.

Some British forest landscape practice relies on the use of
larch to diversify the forest, by highlighting topography
(Crowe, 1978). This recommendation is probably not generally
applicable in Ireland. Although Japanese and Hybrid Larch are
better adapted to Irish climatic conditions than European Larch,
they are intolerant of badly drained sites and very exposed
situations, and their Yield Class here is relatively low (Table I).
While they can be planted on better drained sites, and consequently vary the colour of a forest (e.g. on Tristia, near
Nephin, Co. Mayo), their use is likely to remain limited.
Larches constituted only 3.7% of planting in 1979.

Access and Administration
For initial ploughing, and especially for the extraction of timber
from thinning and felling, forests must be provided with roads.
For administrative purposes, forests are divided into compartments,
which are sometimes separated by rides. The rides provide for
access, and also act as internal fire breaks. An arrangement
of roads following the contours, with rectangular compartments
whose edges and rides run vertically up the hillside, is
intrusive on a steep hillside. While generally acceptable in a
lowland landscape, on open hillsides such a layout "contradicts"
flowing topography. Examples can be seen in Brockagh forest,
Glendalough/Glendasan (where some fire breaks between compartments
are accentuated, visually, by larch planting), in Glendelour,
Slieve Bloom, and high on the south slope of Birreencorragh, Co. Mayo.

A better appearance could be obtained if the roads were
aligned and graded diagonally to the contours. In this
respect the road in the forest west of Lough Inagh, Co. Galway,
looks right. Rides, if possible, should also be curved, and
related to the topography. Such a practice in Britain "is
producing excellent results (Crowe, 1978, p.25). Rides and fire-
breaks should be kept to a minimum for efficient forest management.
If this recommendation is followed, compartments will tend to become
irregularly lozenge-shaped. Ploughing would remain normal to
the slope, so that drains along the roads and rides could act
as collectors to water from the ploughed furrows. The advantages
of such an arrangement of roads and rides, visually, would be that
compartments would screen their neighbours' edges from most
viewpoints and that a basis for irregularly shaped felling coupes
would be designed into the forest from its inception.

FORESTS IN THE DRUMLIN BELT

The landscape of the Leitrim-Cavan-Monaghan drumlin belt is
almost unique in Ireland. It is a small-scale landscape,
dominated by a topography of rather regularly shaped hills,
with a common alignment. Between these, valleys widen into
lakes, or areas of bog. The drumlins have a strong, and
characteristic hedgerow pattern. The landscape is generally
one of strong local enclosure: there are few long views, or
larger hills. Forestry in these areas is notably rare. The
driver is aware of a few forested skylines. Before substantial
afforestation is carried out, it is appropriate to investigate
its possible visual impact. How much afforestation could such
landscapes accept without visual damage? What follows is, to a
degree, speculative, but also an attempt to envisage how
afforestation in such areas may take place.

It appears that afforestation, whether land is acquired by sale
or lease, or planted by the owner, is likely to develop through
the planting of relatively small acreages. The average area
of crops and pasture per holding in most of the three counties is
between 11 and 15 ha. (Gillmor, 1979). In a survey of almost
900 farmers published by Convery and Dripchak (1983), 106 parcels
of land were said to be available for conventional afforestation,
and were surveyed. 28% of the area available (and 78% of the number
of parcels) was in units of 4 hectares of less. The data are
summarised in Table III. Over the three counties, on this basis,
a total of 8.1% of the area would be available for afforestation.
However, if forestry in this area is 'led' by investors, small
acreages may be of relatively little value to them. The minimum

size for an investment forest on such land, depending on yield
class, may be of the order of 15 ha. (Hussey, pers. comm., 1985).
Only some 31% of the area stated to be available was in plots
of this size or greater.

For comparison, data on the grant aiding of private forests in
Galway and Mayo is reproduced in Table IV. Agrarian structure in
these counties is, in general terms (rough grazing excluded),
variously similar to the three counties under review or composed
of even smaller holdings.

If private forestry is investment-led, and if the actual pattern
of availability of land of appropriate area is as above, private
afforestation may be slow to develop. Another matter to consider is
the spatial pattern which private afforestation might take. It might
be random. But it might show a "diffusion" pattern, where an
"innovator" selling, leasing, or planting himself might, in time,
be followed by neighbours. The developing pattern of private forest
around the Mount Callan Tree Farm near Inagh, Co. Clare may exemplify
such a process.

Forestry on wet mineral soils may show some differences from present
conventional practice. The principal tree is likely to be Sitka Spruce.
Rotations, however, may be short - perhaps 30 years. On heavy soils
with impeded drainage windthrow may be a problem. This may be
countered by ripping instead of ploughing. Alternative techniques,
used at Mount Callan Tree Farm, involve ploughing with a single furrow
agricultural plough only. The crop, however, is thinned early

(first thinning at about year 12 on the best soils), heavily
and often (two-year intervals) in order to promote stability.
The principal visual effects of this system relative to conventional forestry, are the parallel "racks" cut in the initial
thinning to extract the timber, and the very much more open
forest. The racks are initially prominent, vertical strips,
achieved by felling two rows at intervals of sixteen rows. These
become less pronounced as the canopies close again, and as further
selective thinning breaks up the mass of the remaining trees.

It is thought that areas of up to perhaps 15-20% of drumlin
areas might be afforested without major change of character. By
about 30% forest cover ("one drumlin in three") the character of the
landscape will be changing significantly. By 50% forest cover, in
a landscape already strongly enclosed, an area of drumlins will begin
to "feel" heavily afforested. This is a gross appreciation of the
process, and the percentages should be taken as approximations only.
Much depends on the pattern of afforestation as it develops. Small
plots on the sides, or crests, of drumlins should be avoided, for
the same visual reasons as elsewhere. It would be preferable for
afforestation to relate to drumlins as basic units, with $1/3$ or $1/2$
a drumlin as a minimum size. Some skyline effects in this landscape
can not realistically be avoided: they will be least where whole
drumlins are planted. Particularly in an area where angling is an
important tourist resource, it will be important to keep access to lake
shores open.

TABLE III - SIZE DISTRIBUTION OF PARCELS SURVEYED IN LEITRIM,
CAVAN AND MONAGHAN

Size of Parcel (Ha.)	Frequency	% of Total Parcels	Total Hectares	% of Total Area
0.4	27	25	11	3
0.8	14	13	11	3
1.2	13	12	16	4
1.6	10	9	16	4
2.0	6	6	12	3
2.4- 4.0	14	13	41	11
4.4- 8.1	10	9	60	16
8.5-16.2	7	7	83	23
16.6-24.3	3	3	58	16
24.7-32.4	2	2	55	15
Totals	106	100	363	100

Source : Convery and Dripchak, 1983, p.36.

TABLE IV - NUMBER OF NEW GRANT-AIDED PRIVATE FORESTS, BY SIZE,
IN GALWAY AND MAYO, 1973-80

Size (Ha.)	
0.5- 4.0	38
4.0- 8.1	5
8.1-12.1	3
12.1-16.2	0
16.2-20.2	1
20.2-24.3	0

Source : Brady Shipman Martin, 1983.

FACTORS OF FOREST MANAGEMENT

Ploughing

To drain the site, and to reduce "weed" competition for the
small transplants used in forestry planting, most forest
sites are ploughed. On upland peatland sites furrows are about
4 metres apart, casting a sod of upturned turf to both sides.
Agricultural type ploughing would give a closer pattern of
plough lines. All ploughing is normal to the slope, to maximise
run off, and for ease of machine working. At close quarters,
such ploughing, especially on the peatland pattern, could be
obtrusive. In practice, the author has seen very little ploughing,
and most of that in background locations. If location decisions
are correct, ploughing is unlikely, in the author's present opinion,
to be obtrusive. It is worth noting that, as planting follows
the ploughed lines, the pattern of ploughing determines the pattern
of the first stage of thinning.

Thinning

Initial thinning is now generally carried out in lines. One
complete line in three or four is removed. This imparts a linear
pattern to the forest, like the initial ploughing, vertically
on the slope. Depending on the rate of growth, it is fairly
short-lived as the canopies close again. It visual impact increases
as slope gradient increases. In comparison with the factors of
initial layout, and with clearfelling, it is not a major factor
in visual impact. As a thinning system, its impact on the wider
landscape is probably less than that of the "racks" required in the

approach developed at Mount Callan. However, care should be
taken if line thinning is to cross a skyline: the resulting
serration would be unsightly. A more selective approach may
be needed in such locations.

Subsequent thinnings are carried out on a selective basis,
to remove the least promising trees. Their visual effect is
progressively to open the forest stand. However, this affects
the internal landscape of the forest more than its appearance
in the wider landscape.

Clearfelling

Clearfelling is already affecting the appearance of some older
forests, and will increase significantly from about 1995. It has
important visual consequences:-

- A "void" is created in the "solid" of a
  mature or maturing forest.
- Surrounding trees are exposed, without side
  branches, and consequently revealing a vertical pattern
  of trunks and a brown-grey colour.
- A litter of "top and lop" covers the forest
  floor. The tops and branches of the trees are cut
  off before the trunks are transported for
  processing. It is uneconomic to remove this
  material, and it does hold a reserve of nutrient
  for the next crop.

The shape of the felling coupe is critical to its impact.
Long straight lines and rectangular shapes should be avoided.
This may be a problem where forests are already laid out in
rectangular compartments, whose margins are relatively windfirm,
and may thus best withstand the removal of adjacent compartments.
The retention of peripheral belts, even if intended for screening,
is best avoided: they may not be windfirm, and, unless very wide,
will tend to look too tall in proportion to their own width,
the scale of the coupe, and the size of the succeeding crop as
it begins to grow. If surrounding trees are to be retained, this
is better done as masses of irregular shape. The shape of the
coupe should be related to the topography, in a similar manner to
that discussed for the layout of the forest.

If a large area of forest is to be felled, it may be done
in stages. The apparent size of the coupe may be reduced by
felling to boldly irregular edges (where these are windfirm).
The stages should be so programmed, if this can be done within
economic constraints, that that next crop is visible in the
first areas felled before the last felling takes place. In some
circumstances, for visual reasons, it may be preferable to fell
trees closest to principal viewpoints last, so as to screen felling
operations. In others it may be best to leave higher areas (where
growth will be slower) until later, by which time a new crop may
be screening, or mitigating, views from below. In detail, the
appearance of a felled area is improved if all broken timber, stumps,
etc. are cut down and removed, and if replanting follows promptly.

Clearfelling, and the initiation of a subsequent rotation,
could afford the opportunity to remedy visually unsatisfactory
features of the initial layout, such as horizontal top margins,
geometric compartments, obstruction of views. However, this
may require a departure from felling at the most finanically
or sylviculturally appropriate time. Interest on the money used
to finance establishment of the plantation is the greatest single
cost in forestry, because of its timescale. The date of felling
is correspondingly important. "The loss of revenue from timber
increases as felling deviates further from the date of maximum
financial return but is not significant within five years" (Lucas,
1983, p.102). If this comment applies to Ireland, it gives some
limited room for adjustment.

FOREST EDGES

Edges to Open Land

However well chosen an acquisition line, or however
sensitively adjusted to topography, the edge of a forest
to open land is likely to appear abrupt. Ancillary features
of the forest edge may strengthen this abruptness, or at least
constrain what may be done to soften it:-

- The forest must be fenced against grazing by
  livestock. Deer fencing is high, and seldom
  used. Most fencing is unobtrusive in itself:
  where close to the edge of a plantation it is
  effectively invisible. Where planting is
  carried up to a fence line, continuously, the
  boundary with open land will be sharp.
  To omit planting over some of the fenced area
  involves a diminution of financial return.
  Planting outside the fence, where circumstances
  would permit, could soften the line, but would
  be exposed to grazing damage. Additional fencing of small
  enclosures is expensive.
- The fence line may, in some circumstances, be
  independent of the forest edge. This means, however,
  that areas of potential moorland grazing are lost,
  and in time the character of the vegetation changes.
  On ungrazed areas heather becomes long and rank,
  grasses thick and tussocky. At close quarters this

can be unsightly, and difficult to walk through.
At a distance the contrast between grazed and
ungrazed areas can show as an arbitrary boundary,
must more intrusive than the fence itself.
-   In some areas a ploughed firebreak is used
to protect a young plantation from fire
driving-in off moorland. It is usually parallel
to the forest edge and fence, and so accentuates the
line of the forest margin.

The treatment of such edges can not be prescribed in general terms:
each must be studied in its context. The following measures, used
alone or in combination, could be adopted:-

-   Where the ground is rocky, and the fence line
independent of the forest edge, "feather" the
planting up between rock outcrops. Leave unplanted, as well, some of the "least plantable"
ground within the forest edge. This type of solution
has been well applied in some forests already
(e.g. north of Lough Dan, Co. Wicklow).
-   Where the forest is close to adjacent deciduous
woodland or scrubland, or to screes and rock
outcrops where deciduous species have survived,
plant groups of the same species in analogous
locations in the forest edge.

- Where the fence line is independent of the planted edge on rather featureless ground, use whatever minor features can be detected to guide a variable plantation edge in a rational way. Plant groups of trees as "outliers".

- Reduce the intensity of cultural operations (e.g. omit ploughing, reduced fertilizing or weeding) in selected areas (not bands) near the fence line, so that growth is slower, and the edge correspondingly less regular.

- Thin early, and heavily in selected areas, retaining the most windfirm trees. Encourage the retention of lateral branches as close as possible to the ground, for appearance and stability. The result would be a more gradual transition to dense forest conditions and, by analogy with conventional shelterbelt design practice, would reduce wind turbulence over the forest edge. Something of the visual effect can be seen in planting which has been damaged by grazing of sheep.

Edges to Roads

Forests are seen at close quarters at roadsides, and where roads pass through them. To most people the appearance of forests from their cars, and their effect on roadside views, may well be more important than their impact in the wider landscape. Along road edges the forest is in a foreground position, and its visual impact very high.

The relationship of forest to road is affected by the following factors:-

- The presence of hedgerows. These are usually present on better quality lowland sites only. They are valuable in retaining the traditional character of the road and in screening the debris of clearfelling at the end of the rotation. However, if trees are planted close to the hedge, they will in time overtop it, and begin to shade it out. The hedge becomes lopsided, and unbalanced when revealed by felling.

- Whether the forest is to both sides of the road or to one side only. In the former case a corridor develops, whose proportion is influenced by the relative set-back of planting from the road edge. Where the road is hedged, and closely planted, a tall, narrow corridor develops as the trees rise above the hedges. As in the previous case, early and heavy thinning is needed close to hedges, to permit then to flourish, and to avoid too constricted a corridor.

- The set back of planting from the road in open land. A set-back of perhaps 6 metres from the road edge avoids too tight a 'corridor', but leaves a strip of unused and unmaintained land. Unless grazed by sheep (as seems to happen at Djouce Woods, Co. Wicklow), the vegetation becomes derelict. Volunteer broadleaf scrub species (Salley and Birch) may seed in, and are to be welcomed in both visual and wildlife conservation

terms. But the overall appearance of such
strips is unsatisfactory.

- The presence of broadleafed trees. Mature
broadleafed trees allow greater visual penetration
than does most coniferous forest, although
mature larch, and mature spruce without lateral
branches can give a similar effect.

- The alignment of the road. A straight road bounded
by tree planting produces a strong formal vista.
A curving alignment produces a greater variety of
light and shade on the road, and on the forest
edge, and a variation in perception of the
forest edge itself.

A special difficulty occurs with 'scenic roads' in forest areas.
Even on steep slopes, the growth of forest crops progressively
obscures views. In the Slieve Bloom this has happened in Glen Regan,
and is happening in Glendine West and Glendelour/Glenmonicknew.
A forest layout that would preserve unobstructed a level line of
sight from a road on a slope of 1 in 3 throughout a 40 year
rotation of Sitka spruce would require a set-back of over 80 metres,
or a loss of 8 hectares of productive land per kilometre of road.
This would be unacceptable, and would raise the question of the
use of the land unplanted.

Forest crops are above eye level for 4/5 or more of the rotation.
There is, therefore, an obvious difficulty in developing scenic
roads through forests which do more than provide views at carefully
selected points.

A solution both to the visual difficulties of corridors and derelict marginal strips, and to the difficulties of scenic routes may lie in a process of design involving two dynamic forces: the movement of vehicles and their passengers along the road, and the growth of the forest, and its management. The landscape of a road through a forest, or passing areas of forest, could be designed and managed to present travellers with a changing sequence of views of the forest itself, and out into the wider landscape. Consistent with road safety and sight distances, setbacks need not, and should not be of uniform width. A constriction of a corridor could precede the emergence of a view over open land. Alternation of forest to left and right, and of open land and views, could be deliberately designed from the point of view of a driver's experience. Something of the kind has happened on the Sally Gap Road, Co. Wicklow westwards to Luggala.

Some areas of ground may have to be kept open to preserve views: these might coincide with areas whose planting would yield least return. Other areas might be managed for short rotation crops (e.g. Noble Fir for Christmas trees). Areas of forest land could provide a sequence, changing with time, of open clearfelled areas, dense young stands, more open, maturing areas (perhaps with heavier thinning than usual), some very tall trees (perhaps retained beyond the point of maximum financial return). Areas of broadleafed trees could be included where they would achieve a specific visual effect - e.g. to highlight a bend in the road. In the abstract the possibilities can only be listed: on each site different approaches and combinations would be appropriate.

ECOLOGICAL IMPACT OF FORESTRY

It is apparent that very little is known of the ecology of
coniferous plantations in Ireland, in terms of their associated
flora and fauna. Deer are reported in some part of 50% of
State forests. Pine Marten and Woodcock are reported to have
increased in numbers (O'Muirgheasa, pers. comm. 1984). An
incomplete sutdy (since abandoned) of woodland and plantations
in the Glendalough area, quoted by Meagher (1982) noted the
following differences in flora:-

Oakwood   :   39 no. species, including those
of the tree canopy.

Larch   :   24 no. of the oakwood species present,
with two additions.

Pine   :   21 no. of the oakwood species present,
with one additional species.

Spruce   :   Only 4 no. species, other than the
spruce itself.

However, it is important to compare like with like. Afforestation
in Glendalough has taken place since 1922. It can not be
expected that plantations would be as rich in associated species
as a semi-natural oakwood of much greater age. Nor is the
age recorded of the forests in which sample plots were taken:
this certainly affects the present of associated species, primarily
through control of light intensity at ground level. Seedlings of
deciduous woodland species have been observed in a well thinned,

privately owned plantation near Inagh, Co. Clare, in which
more light reaches the forest floor than under more conventional
management. Perhaps due to disturbance from continued thinning
they have not generally persisted.

However, with the above reservations in mind, plantations
of non-indigenous species, grown on relatively short rotations,
are probably rather poor in associated species. Under
conventional management, the period from the time when the
canopy closes until it is opened by successive thinnings (from
about 25 years old onwards), the internal woodland environment
is dark. In later years light levels increase: a dense ground
flora of bramble was noted under mature Norway Spruce at
Killykeen, Co. Cavan. However, the rotational system is unlikely
to give enough stability in the woodland environment to allow a
complex associated flora to develop, except along external and
internal edges where light levels remain higher, and where variable
plant habitats may be created by degrees of shelter and drainage.

The habitat of coniferous plantations should be further considered
in the context of a fully developed forest, containing, in different
areas, a variety of age classes. Doyle and Moore (1982) studied
the transition of vegetation following ploughing and afforestation
on deep blanket peat in Glenamoy forest, Co. Mayo. The pattern
showed, after drainage, an initial rapid diminution of bog species,
with increased vigour of Calluna and the purple moor-grass, Molinia
caerulea. Species normally associated with Calluna-dominated
vegetation increased. As the tree canopy closed, some species
considered typical of acidophilous oakwood in the west of Ireland

were observed to be present. Many of these, however, were
absent again in older plantations with a closed canopy. In
areas clearfelled, a new flora of light-demanding species will
develop, until the subsequent crop closes canopy.

There is scope for research, over a period of time, and in
forests of different ages, to establish their relative value
as a habitat for wildlife. The value of such a habitat would
seem to depend not simply on a number of plant species present,
but also on the structures of the vegetation (the numbers of
"layers" between canopy and ground level), shelter, nesting sites,
food resources, and the presence of rare species, if any.

Without such detailed research, a few general propositions may
be advanced as the basis of policy:-

- Most coniferous afforestation in upland
  areas has probably involved little
  loss of value for wildlife (plants and
  animals). The existing vegetation of
  such areas is usually characterized by
  a few, common species. Afforestation
  may diversify this in terms of both
  species and structure.
- The principle 'casualty' of afforestation
  of marginal agricultural land is likely
  to be the loss of hedgrows, through shading.
  Otherwise, relatively little loss of value
  may be envisaged.

- In both these cases, however, if
areas of different vegetation occur,
such as scrub woodland or salley/alder
fringes to lakes and rivers, or other
wetland, these should be retained, to
diversify the forest habitat.

- There should be a general presumption
against the conversion to coniferous
forest of rich natural or semi-natural
ecosystems (e.g. the remaining semi-natural
oakwoods), or representatives of
scientifically interesting or threatened
ecosystems (unmodified raised bog, some
unmodified blanket bog) (Doyle, in press).

- Such areas retained should be deliverately
managed to conserve, if not to increase,
their value as wildlife habitat. In
comparison with the well developed skills
of commercial forest management, there
may be a need for further development of
skills in this area.

THE ROLE OF BROADLEAVES

Ireland's original forest cover was based on broadleaf species,
with Scots Pine at an early post-glacial stage and in the uplands
until 'drowned' by developing blanket bog. In terms of their
associated flora and fauna, if properly managed, broadleaf woodlands
have a higher value for wildlife conservation than commercial
coniferous forests are likely to have. It is notable that the
(British) Foresty Commission publication Wildlife Conservation in
Woodlands (1972) and the Irish material reviewed by Meagher (1982,
pp.117-121, 188-200) are substantially concerned with broadleaf
species.

There is no evidence that broadleafed species could be a commercial
crop if planted in Ireland today, at least on the quality of
land heretofore available. If they were, their management as a
crop would not necessarily produce the species-rich environment
of old semi-natural woodland. Broadleaves as an element in
coniferous forests can be justified only on visual or conservation
grounds.

It is important, however, to note the limitations of
certain British recommendations in this field when applied to
Ireland (Crowe, 1978). British landscapes appear to be better
endowed with broadleaf woodland than their Irish counterparts.
It is therefore easier in Britain to use broadleaf trees to link
forests into the existing landscape than in Ireland. In Ireland,
also, a relatively large proportion of planting has been on acid
peatlands. Of common broadleaf species, only birch and salley
thrive on such sites.

Broadleafed trees, therefore, should be planted only for specific visual and wildlife conservation purposes.

As an element in forest design, they may be consciously used to improve its appearance in terms of contrast, accent and modelling, where permitted by soil conditions. Such applications could include:-

- To highlight the course of a stream in an otherwise solidly planted valley. This could preserve the 'flow' of the landscape referred to earlier.
- To highlight particular features of topography (e.g. rocky knolls), or a bend in a road.
- To diversify the forest margin at the waterside, especially if the water level fluctuates. (note the extensive salley/alder scrub in the woodland edges of Killykeen and Cootehill forests).

The appropriate and successful use of broadleaves requires a conscious search for appropriate sites, as part of the forest design. Their use as 'amenity strips' in screening is an un-satisfactory approach. Coniferous forests ought to be designed and managed primarily in their own terms. If this is done, they need not be concealed. Attempts at such concealment are prone to overlooking. The (too) widespread use of Lyeland cypress hedging, the older tradition of small farm shelter plantations, and the relatively absence of a "conifers vs. open land" debate such as occurs in Britain, all suggest that opposition to coniferous trees as such is unlikely to be widespread.

Broadleaf trees grow relatively slowly. They need, therefore, to be managed on their own terms. They should be planted in groups large enough for them to grow properly, and managed so that their crowns can develop. Deciduous trees grown, or tolerated, in mixtures with conifers appear frail, narrow-crowned and drawn up if retained beyond the end of the conifer rotation. Conifers should not, then, be interplanted with deciduous trees, unless as an early 'nurse'. Conifer crops surrounding broadleaves should be thinned as necessary so as not to dominate them. Such an approach ought to maximise the conservation value of broad-leafed trees, by providing long-term stability, and an opportunity for an associated flora to develop.

THE INTERNAL FOREST LANDSCAPE

Forests have an internal landscape, analogous to the
'townscape' of urban settlements. It is this internal
landscape which is a prime resource for recreation. Some of
the considerations applied to scenic roads apply here also,
but the F.W.S. favours non-motorized recreation in its forests,
so that the scale and speed at which the landscape is viewed
differs.

The internal forest landscape varies according to the following
factors:-

-    The crop: its age (and therefore height), its
     management (affecting its density), and species
     (affecting growth habit, colour and
     texture).
-    The underlying topography, principally slope,
     and its associated features: rock outcrops, water-
     courses, lakes.
-    Relics of older landscapes, e.g. old trees, buildings,
     hedgerows.
-    The quality of forest roads and paths: their width,
     alignment and gradient.

Commercial forest itself, under conventional management, is in many
ways an unexciting landscape for recreation:-

-    Trees are above eye level for some 4/5 of the
     rotation, so preventing outward views except
     along sloping roads and over steeply falling contours.

-       The closed tree canopy, until first thinning
        at least, excludes light and visual
        penetration.

-       Only in the later stages of the rotation does
        the forest below the canopy open significantly,
        so that a forest floor vegetation can
        develop.

-       Forest roads, if long and straight, broad and
        level, can be relatively tedious for walking,
        in comparison with the smaller, faster changing
        scale of footpaths.

Some of these effects may be changed by forest management. Areas
can be felled for viewpoints. The appearance of the forest itself
may be radically altered by management measures. The thinning
regime of Mount Callan Tree Farm described above, undertaken for
strictly sylvicultural reasons, produces a much more open stand
early in the rotation. This is, however, on relatively good soil.
It is also accompanied by early selection of the final crop trees,
and pruning of lateral branches. In State forests pruning has seldom
been done. The need for it, and its commercial justification,
are subjects of debate. If it is undertaken, the landscape of the
forest would benefit. There may, in any case, be "a greater move
towards wider spacing, early and heavy thinning, and pruning, at
least under some circumstances of species and site". (O'Carroll,
1984, p.62).

The principal recreational value of a forest probably lies
in features associated with its topography, and previous history,
outward views, and areas of wildlife conservation interest.
This is clearly recognised in the facilities provided at existing
State forests. Perhaps the next step (where this too is not
already done) is to identify these features at the design stage
of the forest, and so to incorporate provision for recreational
use into its design and management policies from the beginning.
The consequences which would flow from such a policy could include
design of the forest along watercourses for recreational use,
the planting of broadleafed species for maximum recreational
and conservation advantage, or the identification of areas which
might be kept open and managed for a different use (picnicing,
or hay meadow).

FOREST, LANDSCAPE AND DESIGN

The tendency of current commercial forestry practice is to
introduce a production system of rather uniform characteristics
into a diversity of existing Irish landscapes. To the extent
that forestry becomes visually significant in these landscapes,
there is a loss of regional landscape diversity. An appraisal,
therefore, of these landscapes, and the design of forests so
as to acommodate them as sympathetically as possible, are both
required. The preceding sections have reviewed the visual
impact of the forests in terms of their layout and management,
and at different scales of appreciation. It is the task of landscape
analysis and landscape design to examine the probable impact of
proposed afforestation, to identify design and management measures
required to fit the forest to the landscape, to conservation and
recreation objectives, and to relate these to the afforestation
plan and programme of operations. A thorough analysis of the
existing landscape is a pre-requisite for this process; an
analysis of topography, hydrology, soil, vegetation, and visual
characteristics. Some of these factors are part of normal forestry
site appraisal. Others, it would appear, are not. Design is
a positive process, by which the rather negative reasoning inherent
in visual impact assessment is reversed, and changed into an effort
to produce the best result for the landscape within technical
and financial constraints.

In the course of perparation of this study, it has been
concluded that most Irish landscapes can accept afforestation,
provided that it is properly and sympathetically designed. Where
the basis of the landscape is dramatic topography, the scale of

the forests should not become so large as to dominate it.
However, there are some landscapes where there should probably
be a presumption against further afforestation. A complete list
cannot be given, and the recommendations here should not be
considered final. An interim list would include the following:-

Lowland south Connemara, west of about Maam Cross:
This is a landscape of great subtlety. Topography is
small-scale and varied, with abundant small lakes.
Colours are subtle and varied. In a landscape of low
relief the sky is of great importance. Forestry, where
it has taken place, very easily dominates the scale of
this landscape. Forest edges read as rather strong
lines. It is a landscape of considerable cultural
and tourist significance and merits the most careful
conservation.

The Burren: A limestone landscape unique in western
Europe, and of great value for its flora. Planting
could not realistically be proposed for the limestone
plateaux. However, the contrast of pasture and scrub
in the valleys and basins is important to the quality
of the overall landscape. Afforestation here would
damage this quality.

North Mayo Blanket Bog: This landsape may justify
a presumption against forestry on the grounds of its
unique scale as a lowland blanket bog landscape. However,
there may also be a case for afforestation of bog cutover for the E.S.B. Bellacorick Generating Station.

REGULATION

Development Control?

Should the Planning Acts be amended so that forestry is
defined as 'Development'? At first sight there are some grounds
for so doing:-

- Afforestation involves a long-term change in
the use and appearance of land, often of large
areas, and in scenic locations.

- Afforestation may alter the employment pattern
of an area, in complex ways and at different stages
of the rotation cycle.

- Afforestation may lead to "downstream" developments
in timber processing.

- Afforestation requires "development" works such
as roading, and may generate traffic of large
vehicles ill-suited to local road
networks.

- Private afforestation, particularly in its
location, is now controlled only to the extent that
grant aid is dicretionary.

There are, however, arguments against such a change of law:-

- Depending on how the law were drafted, the
positions of State and private afforestation with
respect to it could differ. The justice of discrimination
between two types of commercial enterprise is
questionable. Were State afforestation included, it
would add another layer of official control to an
already bureaucratic process.

- The procedures involved would interfere
  with land acquisition, already a complex matter.
  Even though planning applications would prudently
  be made by prospective purchasers, the timescale
  of acquisition would be extended, and the
  risk of fruitless site appraisal
  increased.

- Afforestation would have to be very widespread
  and dramatic significantly to affect local employment
  within the timescale of a county development plan.
  Processing industries would be the subject of
  separate planning applications. Large vehicles
  already use rural roads in connection with agricultural
  activities, such as milk collection and
  drainage.

- The principal concerns surrounding most afforestation
  projects are visual. Planners' education does not
  include systematic training in this area. Nor are
  they familiar with the techniques and requirements
  of forestry.

- The practice of forestry, and its visual impact,
  involves not simply initial layout, but a series of
  management operations. The control of such a system
  would be complex and difficult.

- If the primary arguments for planning control of
  forestry are visual, these would be tenuous grounds,
  of necessity subjective even if rational, on which
  to control a productive use of land.

It is therefore considered that, on balance, planning control should not be extended to afforestation. This conclusion leaves the private sector without accountability, except through the 'lever' of discretionary grant aid. However, it should be borne in mind that:-

- Most private afforestation to date has been on a small scale, and control of much of this activity could be as vexatious to planners as to the landowners involved.
- The areas of land of greatest interest to investment foresters are not, except for the drumlin belt, generally likely to be in scenic landscapes. Within the drumlin belt, the pattern of land holding, and the process of its release for afforestation, so far as it can be envisaged, are unlikely to lead to extensive and continuous forests in the reasonably near future.

The general aims of the Forest and Wildlife Service, quoted by O'Carroll (1984, p.114) are to promote:-

- "Sound national forest and wildlife policies.
- A patterns of land use so adjusted that both forestry and wildlife will yield the greates benefits, taking into account the national economic and social policies, including environmental, industrial and employment considerations.

-       The development of a comprehensive programme

        for wildlife conservation".

Two of eight objectives flowing from these aims are:-

-       "The development of suitable forest areas for

        amenity, recreation and public

        education".
-       "Wildlife conservation and improvement of

        game stock".

The Forest and Wildlife Service publishes no documents on its
landscape policy.   It has, however, been argued that "It is
evident, nevertheless, that a strong, though unpublished recreation
and landscape management policy does exist" (Kennedy and McCusker,
1983, p.222). In the light of some of the evidence noted in
earlier sections, it is doubtful whether there exists an adequate
landscape policy, well formulated and applied, addressing the
fundamental issues of forest design. Certainly the objective on
amenity, recreation and public eduction would not cover such a
landscape policy.

A Code of Practice?
In the context of a developing private forestry industry, the whole
burden of a landscape policy ought not to fall on the Forest
and Wildlife Service. Especially in the light of its freedom
from planning control, the private forestry sector has responsibilities
also. It is considered that self-regulation of the forestry
industry, soundly based, is more likely to achieve satisfactory
integration of forests into the landscape than planning control:-

- Most of the problems to be addressed
  are matters of design. They are not, on the
  whole, particularly complex. Most are such
  that foresters, with experience, some training,
  and adequate information could solve
  for themselves.
- The solutions to problems of visual impact have
  to be implemented, in both forest design and
  management by foresters.
- The visual implications of afforestation need to
  be envisaged before land is acquired. Once a
  sale has been concluded, location is fixed and
  room for adjustment is severely limited.

At present the F.W.S. has Amenity Officers to advise on those
aspects of forestry. This approach is probably too limited.
Awareness of landscape issues in afforestation should extend from
inspectors working on land acquisition, to district and divisional
inspectors, to forest engineers, to forest officers, to private
forestry consultants, forest owners and investors. It is therefore
recommended that a Code of Practice for Forest Landscape be
prepared by the forestry industry, with assistance, to make the
necessary information widely available. It could cover the kinds
of issues identified here, and techniques to resolve them. It might
also cover areas where there would be a presumption against
afforestation, and guidance as to when specialist advice should be
obtained.

The forest industry may fear to make "a rod for its own back".
It could be argued that, if public pressure were to build
up as a result of unsympathetic afforestation or forest practice,
the rod's application would be justified. The converse of this
situation would be that a good forest landscape policy, well
implemented, could help to ensure the public's acceptance of,
and support for, forestry, especially as it extends down from
the uplands and closer to the everyday lives of a greater number
of people.

Landscape Objectives

A final recommendation relates specifically to the Forest and
Wildlife Service. With the definition of prime acquisition areas,
the location of future forestry development is, or should be,
more certain that it formerly was. The pace of development is
still uncertain. Expansion of clearfelling, often in these same
general areas, is expected from the 1990's, if not before. It is,
therefore, suggested that it is now a particularly appropriate
time to formulate landscape objectives for the larger F.W.S. land
holdings, and areas of potential acquisition. Such objectives
would provide a context for the further development of forestry
in these areas. Given uncertain timescales, they could probably
not be formalized into definite landscape plans. Like the proposed
Code of Practice, the "objectives" would be concerned with the
application of the considerations discussed in this paper, but to
specific situations. In so doing, they could guide the future
evolution of some important parts of the Irish rural landscape.

Acknowledgements

I am indebted to many foresters, in both the State and private sectors, for their help in preparing this paper. Responsibility for any errors, and for all opinions unless specifically attributed, is my own.

References

Anon.	Building on Reality, Dublin, 1984.
Brady Shipman Martin	West Region Study : Development Strategy to 2004 : Vol. 2 : Report of Survey. West Regional Development Organisation and Commission of the European Communities, 1983.
Bulfin, M.	'Forestry and the Irish Farmer'. Paper read at conference, Energy Potential in Development of Irish Forestry, U.C.G., 13th April, 1984.
Campbell, D.	'Landscape Design Considerations in Large Scale Forestry Operations in Great Britain' in Planning Outlook, 20, 2 (1977), pp.6-14.
Convery, F. J.	Irish Forestry Policy (NESC Paper No. 46) Dublin, 1979.
Convery, F.J. and Dripchak, F.	Energy Crops, Forestry and Regional Development in Ireland (ESRI Paper No. 114). Dublin, 1983.
Crowe, S.	The Landscape of Forests and Woods (Forestry Commission Booklet No. 44), London, 1978.
Doyle, G.J.	'Protecting Irish Turf Moors'. Paper read to Conseil International de la Chasse et de la Conservation du Gibier, Paris, 1984. In press.
Doyle, G.J. and Moore, J.J.	'Floristic Changes in Developing Conifer Plantations Growing on Blanket Peat in the West of Ireland' in Struktur und Dynamik von Waldern: Berichte der Internationalen Symposien der Internationalen Vereinigung fur Vegetationskunde. Braunschweig, 1982, pp. 699 - 716.

Farrell, E.P.

'Land Acquisition for Forestry' in Blackwell, J. and Convery F.J., <u>Promise and Performance: Irish Environmental Policies Analyzed</u>. Dublin, 1983, pp.155 - 167.

Forrest and Wildlife Service

<u>The Case for Forestry</u>, Dublin, 1980 / 83.

Gillmor, D.A.

'Agriculture' in Gillmor, D.A. (Ed.), <u>Irish Resources and Land Use</u>, Dublin 1979.

Industrial Development Authority

<u>Developing the Irish Timber Industry for the '80's</u>. Dublin, 1981.

Kennedy, J.J. and McCusker, P.

'State Forest Amenity Policies for a Growing Urban Irish Population' in Blackwell, J. and Convery, F.J., <u>Promise and Performance: Irish Environmental Policies Analyzed</u>, Dublin, 1983, pp. 219 - 228.

Lucas, O.W.R.

'The Landscape Design of Forestry' in <u>Planning Outlook</u>, 26, 2 (1983), pp 98 - 104.

Meagher, F.

<u>The Implications of Forestry for Rural Planning</u>. Unpublished Master's Thesis, U.C.D., 1981.

O'Carroll, N (Ed).

<u>The Forests of Ireland</u>, Dublin, 1984.

O'Loughlin, B.

'Investment Potential of Irish Forestry'. Paper read at Conference, <u>Energy Potential in Development of Irish Forestry</u>, U.C.G., 13th April 1984.

Royal Irish Academy

<u>Atlas of Ireland</u>, Dublin, 1979.

Steele, R.C.

<u>Wildlife Conservation in Woodlands</u> (Forestry Commission Booklet No. 29), London, 1972.

CHANGING PEATLAND LANDSCAPES

Shier, C.W. and McNally, G.

INTRODUCTION - MIRE TYPES IN IRELAND

Peatlands occupy 1.34 million hectares in Ireland, covering 16.2% of the land surface. Within the Irish Republic they cover 1.17 million hectares, which is equivalent to 17.2% of the land area. Peatlands (mires) may be divided into three main groups in Ireland: the raised bogs, blanket bogs and fens.

The raised bogs are concentrated mainly in the Central Plain, from Kildare across to East Galway and Mayo, and from Sligo south to Tipperary. They may be sub-divided into a True Midland Type and a Western or Intermediate Type, on the basis of morphology, surface pattern and vegetation, but for landscape purposes we may treat these sub-types as a single unit. They originally occupied an area of 311,000 ha, of which some 246,000 ha or 79% has been modified by man in various ways.

Blanket bog is a climatic mire type which forms under specific conditions of cool summers, high rainfall and high humidity. It is found in Ireland in areas which experience precipitation in excess of 1250mm and more than 225 rain days per year. Irish blanket bogs may be divided into two sub-types:

(i)   the low-level, Atlantic Type blanket bogs, which occur below
        152 m O.D. and are found along the western seaboard, mainly in

Donegal, West Mayo, Galway and Kerry. They occupy 336,000 ha, of which 27% has been man modified to date.

(ii) The high-level, Montane Type blanket bogs, which occur above the 152m level and are found in Donegal, Sligo, from Clare down to South Cork and also on mountain groups further east, particularly the Wicklow Mountains, the Slieve Blooms, and the Galty, Knockmealdown, Comeragh and Monavullagh Mountains. Montane blanket bog occupies 437,000 ha, of which 25% has been designated man modified.

The final peatland type, fen, occurs mainly on lowland sites throughout the country and differs markedly from the preceding bog types in both vegetation and hydrology. Originally occupying some 92,000 ha, practically all of our fen areas have been either partially or completely reclaimed and modified (Hammond, 1979).

PEATLAND LANDSCAPES

Fens develop from bodies of open water, which gradually infill through deposition of the initial floating and emergent aquatic species. Over time this allows the colonisation of semi-terrestial plants and a natural progression to fen carr and wet woodland. At all stages the vegetation is in direct contact with, and is strongly influenced by, the minerotrophic groundwater.

Fens in Ireland are not large enough to be considered a characteristic landscape in their own right, but rather form elements within the landscape. They are flat, open to partially enclosed, depending on the stage of succession, and vary in colour from dull greens in summer to pale browns in winter.

Continued seral succession of fens in Ireland, with unconfined peat deposition above the influence of groundwater, has resulted in the formation of our raised bogs.

Raised bogs which have their origin in the basins of Post-glacial lakes are almost circular in outline, while those which developed along the floodplains of our major rivers are more longitudinal in nature. Except for a few of the larger Midland complexes, where the peatland appears to stretch endlessly almost to the horizon, the raised bogs should also be considered as a landscape element, occupying depressions between the hills and eskers and contrasting with the surrounding enclosed mineral areas.

Raised bogs are open, slightly domed in morphology, have a rough texture, owing to the presence of vegetation hummocks and small pools on the surface, and vary seasonally from golden brown to green and purple.

In the climatic blanket bogs of the west and mountains the landscape character is determined by the bog itself. A relatively uniform blanket of peat follows the topography, reflecting the underlying geomorphology, with individual features such as rivers, rock outcrops or lakes clearly pronounced. The landscape is open, treeless, characterised by wide views, a rough surface texture and changing seasonal colours.

CURRENT UTILISATION OF THE PEATLANDS

Fuel Production

Hand cutting of peat for fuel results in the intrusion of drainage channels, edges, vertical banks, or in other words straight elements, into an essentially non-linear landscape. Hand winning of peat has been practiced throughout recorded history, but accelerated in the 17th century following clearance of most of the native forests. Considering that around 5 million tonnes of fuel peat, almost equivalent to what Bord na Mona is producing today, was produced annually in the 18th and 19th centuries, some idea of the enormous depletion of the original peatland resource may be gained.

Hand-cutover areas, which traditionally suffer the limitation of inadequate drainage, are frequently abandoned and undergo natural recolonisation. Some areas may be used for rough grazing, with little or no management input, while others are reclaimed all the way to more productive ley grassland.

Recent advances in the design and production of light, simple, tractor-attached sod peat production machinery have resulted in an increase in the acreage of peatlands under private fuel production. This includes the development of new areas, and the re-utilisation of formerly abandoned areas in both the raised bogs and blanket peatlands.

Industrial production of fuel and horticultural peat by Bord na Mona has a significant impact on the peatland landscape, especially in the Midlands. This industrial activity results in the imposition of geometric drainage and production layouts, total removal of the original vegetation, with attendant colour and textural changes, and the intrusion of the necessary production and utilisation hardware, such as railways, bridges, machines, power stations etc. The landscape impact may be viewed as transient since cutover peatland areas will be redeveloped for alternative land uses and reintegrated with the surrounding land structure upon cessation of peat production operations.

Agriculture

Agricultural reclamation of peatlands in Ireland is primarily to grassland, often with the remnants of naturally colonised Betula or Salix forming intermittent hedges and windbreaks along field boundaries. The colour, texture and overall structure blends with adjoining mineral areas, although the latter frequently exhibit a higher degree of enclosure.

In many areas, especially on the blanket bogs, there are natural limits beyond which agricultural reclamation is not economically viable. The reclamation of peatlands in Ireland for agriculture has in general been limited by a combination of ownership complications, insufficient arterial drainage, a lack of local technical expertise and a traditional no-risk approach (van Eck, 1984).

Rough grazing of cattle and sheep occurs on all peatland types, and on Midland cutover areas this practice leads to the maintenance of diverse mixtures of coarse grasses, perennials and scrub, while on blanket bog little change in the natural flora is discernable under light stocking. Heavy trampling leads to a reduction in species

diversity and in montane areas may accelerate erosion of unstable
blanket peats.

Forestry

Afforestation of peatlands in Ireland is carried out primarily by the
State, with very little private forestry planted on peatland to date.
Some 170,000 hectares, or 51% of the total state forest, is on peatland, mainly on blanket bogs in the western counties (O'Carroll,
1984). Afforestation with coniferous species effectively encloses
these open peatland landscapes, shrouding the geomorphology and
introducing striking changes in colour and texture. Unsympathetic
planting and management regimes have resulted in the imposition of
rigid lines and angular blocks on some sections of the naturally
contoured or rugged peatland landscape.

Conservation

1970 marked European Conservation year, which gave the initial impetus
for peatland conservation in Ireland, and since then a little progress
has been made in the conservation of representative examples of our
main peatland types. Three small areas totalling 112 ha are
protected in entirety, while parts of seven other peatland areas
are also protected (Ryan and Cross, 1984).

Several of these areas are protected through acquisition and
consolidation by Bord na Mona with subsequent title transferral to
bodies such as An Taisce or the Forest and Wildlife Service (FWS),
while others occur within designated National Parks which are
administered by the Office of Public Works (OPW) - see Table 1.

Site	Peatland Type	Total Area (ha)	Area Protected (ha)	Protecting Agency
Pollardstown, Co Kildare	Fen	225	78	FWS
Bellacorrick, Co Mayo	Fen	30	30	An Taisce
Raheenmore, Co Offaly	Raised Bog	190	168	FWS
Mongan, Co Offaly	Raised Bog	215	125	An Taisce
Owenbeagh, Co Donegal	Intermediate	17	17	OPW
Newfoundland, Co Kerry	Intermediate	65	65	OPW
Roundstone, Co Galway	Western Blanket Bog	4250	865	OPW
Pettigo Plateau, Co Donegal	Western Blanket Bog	1620	890	FWS
Slieveblooms, Co Laois/Offaly	Montane Blanket Bog	3100	2400	FWS
Mangerton, Co Kerry	Montane Blanket Bog	2000	1000	OPW

Table 1.   - Location, Type and Area of Peatlands Protected at Present

INDUSTRIALLY CUTOVER PEATLANDS

Before one can anticipate what the landscapes of the present industrial bogs will look like in the future one has to consider the technical and economic limitations. In order to do so it is necessary to understand the sequence of peat formation in the Post-glacial era.

In the Midland raised bogs peat formation has taken place over two distinctive soil groups (Carey and Hammond, 1970).

a) Developed Soils

Well developed relict soils are derived from limestone boulder till on the higher contours of the bog floor. These soils exhibit a higher degree of profile development which can be attributed to the period of exposure during which they were subjected to soil forming processes.

b) Undeveloped Soils

These soils are in general classified as calcareous deep silts and silty clays on the lower levels of the bog floor. Formed under limnic conditions these soils were not exposed to weathering processes and are characterised by a lack of stones, gravels or boulders, a fine silt to silty clay texture, massive structure, slightly plastic consistence and grey colour. In certain circumstances, deposits of shell marl and calcareous muds can be found to varying depths overlying these silty clay deposits.

Initial peat formation at the lower contours of the bog floor resulted from the accumulated remains of Phragmites and other aquatics. Over the millennia, peat began to accumulate at inter-mediate levels and this peat is generally of wood fen origin. The peat lying on the higher contours of the bog floor consists of woody debris from the Post-glacial forests (Barry, 1969).

Thus, following peat extraction for fuel by Bord na Mona, three main peat types make up the residual peat to a depth of approx-imately 0.5m. As a broad general rule, we can say that forest debris peat overlies the well developed relict soils, that wood fen peat overlies the moderately developed soils and that peat of limnic origin overlies the silty clays of the lower contours.

Factors which have to be taken into account when deciding on future cutover peatland utilisation include:

(1) Peat type

(2) Subsoil type

(3) Bog floor contour levels and their relationship to the arterial drainage of the surrounding area

(4) Intensity of local drainage

Within any raised bog unit, the original peat depth can vary from 3m to 10m. As peat extraction takes place mainly in a horizontal manner by the milled peat process, the time scale for cutaway emergence is widespread even within any one bog area, requiring up to twenty years before all sections are completly cut out.

It is not desirable to leave the cutover areas for this time period as they rapidly colonise with scrub and incur a higher reclamation cost. However, if random areas are reclaimed as they emerge their utilisation poses several problems, particularly if the option chosen is grassland, because an infrastructure of buildings and services is an integral part of grassland farming in Ireland.

Experience gained from pilot work to date

Research and development work to date by Bord na Mona has concentrated on the better peat types overlying well developed relict soils, except for one project based on cutover blanket peat in the west. In the initial years of experimentation, grass and other crops were sown directly onto the residual peat with the minimum of distrubance to the underlying subsoil. Major problems, however, were encountered with this approach (Healy, 1980):

(i) The higher contours of the bog floor were afforested prior to peat formation and the peat overlying these sites contains large residues of fossil timber. As the peat settles and shrinks the fossil timber becomes exposed and causes major problems with harvesting of crops.

(ii) The low permeability interface between the peat and subsoil restricts vertical movement of water which in turn leads to trafficability problems.

(iii) Inadequate lime incorporation leads to poor rooting and subsequently reduced yields during periods of low rainfall.

Therefore, for utilisation other than commercial forestry, the cutover area is now developed in the following manner:-

Year 1 - The residual peat (0.5m) together with 15 cm of the subsoil (depth to which decalcification has usually taken place) is deep ploughed. The exposed fossil timber is removed and the area is then left to undergo weathering processes for a period of at least twelve months.

Year II - The peat and subsoil are thoroughly mixed, during suitable weather conditions, and the area is levelled and allowed to settle.

Year III - The area is finally levelled, cultivated and prepared for sowing.

It was formerly thought that this development period could be shortened by sowing cereals in year II, but unripened cutover peatland has proved an unsuitable medium for cereal production (MacNaeidhe et al, 1980). Trials are under way at the moment to assess the possible role of oil-seed rape in this initial development.

Highly productive permanent grassland can be established by this reclamation procedure. In the Board's commercial developments grass has been utilised for beef production and in latter years for a combination of beef and lamb production. Production levels on reclaimed peatlands are at the top end of the scale of Irish production for these products (Drennan et al, 1984).

Technical competence alone is not sufficient, as other factors will determine whether or not an area is developed for grassland. The greatest economic constraint is the cost of infrastructure provision, including overwintering facilities for animals, road structure, electricity and water services and stock fencing. Obviously, the greater the intensity of infrastructure the smaller the scale of landscape created and the higher the reclamation cost per hectare.

To date, no substantial areas of peat overlying undeveloped soils have reached the cutover stage. Drainage research on these low-permeability, silty clay soils is being conducted on one small area and early indications suggest that agricultural reclamation costs will be double those of weathered soils at higher contours.

Major technical problems were encounted with establishing and maintaining grassland on cutover blanket bog in the west of Ireland, and after ten years experience it has been concluded that grassland enterprises are not an economical proposition on this peat type.

Coniferous Forestry on Cutover Peatlands

Ireland's climate is very suitable for forestry and growth rates are among the highest in Europe. Sitka Spruce and Lodgepole Pine are the

species of most significance in peatland forestry and cutover areas
are potentially the most productive peatland sites. Experimental
plantations on Bord na Mona cutover bog at Clonsast, Co. Offaly
indicate that potential yields of both Sitka Spruce and Lodgepole Pine
are over 20 m^3 per hectare per annum.

Fuel peat production layouts on the bogs favour subsequent afforestation by lowering establishment costs. However, owing to the highly
alkaline nature of the subsoils, excessive removal of peat could
render these areas unsuitable for coniferous forestry, and a minimum
peat depth of 50cm must be retained in all potential forestry areas.

Utilisation of Cutover for Amenity Purposes

Development plans for cutover peatland areas must recognise society's
growing leisure activities and the increasing emphasis on amenity,
education and recreation. These require diversity, balance and
interest in the landscape and are unlikely to be satisfied by mono-
cultural softwood forests or open prairies.

Areas which require pumped drainage to facilitate peat harvesting
will ultimately yield cutover comprising lower peats and undeveloped
relict soils, on which neither agriculture nor forestry may be
economically viable if pumping has to be maintained. Such areas may
be more usefully flooded and developed towards fish farming,
recreation and wildlife conservation.

Particular attention will have to be focused on cutover development
in two regions:

i) The eastern bogs which lie within day-trip radius of the huge
   Dublin conurbation.

ii) The bogs of the Shannon Basin, an area of great vacational development potential, especially attractive to foreign tourists.

The main conclusions from work carried out to date suggest that grass-land, forestry or a combination of both is the most likely use for cutover peatland overlying the upper contours of the bog floor. The potential of the lower contour peats is not yet clearly identified, but options other than agriculture or forestry are likely to dominate future developments.

THE FUTURE OF OTHER PEATLAND AREAS.

Industrial extraction of peat, on around 80,000 hectares of consolidated land holdings, facilitates integrated planning and allows an assessment of the potential long-term landscape impacts, but what of the much larger peatland area owned and worked by the private sector?

With continued mechanisation of sod peat production, hand-cutting of peat fuel is likely to decline further, as machines replace the required hard labour on all but the steepest montane slopes, or in areas where traditional practices are maintained, perhaps for the sake of turf-cutting competitions. The recent proliferation of relatively simple, tractor-powered machines will also accelerate the development and opening up of new production areas, especially the smaller Western raised bogs, and the deeper, uniform areas of blanket bog on gentle slopes.

The potential for reclamation following peat extraction will again depend on the local hydrology and on the depth and nature of the residual peat. But what if the operator simply abandons the site?

In the raised bogs of the Midlands recolonisation will mirror what is apparent today following centuries of hand extraction. Areas of moderately deep, acidic peat will colonize initially with <u>Calluna</u> or <u>Molinia</u>, eventually yielding light <u>Betula</u> scrubland. Areas of shallow peat, especially where the underlying glacial drift exerts an influence, will colonise initially with grasses, sedges and rush, which quickly succeeds to <u>Betula</u>, <u>Salix</u>, and <u>Sorbus</u>, and eventually to mixed woodland.

In the blanket bogs, cutover areas recolonise with a modified form of the original flora, which over a long period of time may become virtually indistinguishable from the original, provided alteration of the prevailing hydrology has not been too severe.

Agriculture

Grassland enterprises are the most successful agricultural systems on reclaimed peatlands. However, with limits already on dairy production, we are unlikely to see any great expansion of these enterprises on peat in the future, unless demand and prices for animal-based products show substantial changes on the international market. High reclamation costs, poor returns and the slow but significant change in western diet, away from high-calorie, saturated fatty foods, are unlikely to encourage private investment in this area.

Tillage practices in Ireland have already moved off the more marginal soils, and it is likely that grassland enterprises will tend to follow, with further consolidation and intensification as margins and returns become leaner. Midland peat areas which are reclaimed to grassland in the future may not, therefore, have to integrate with the existing enclosed, small-scale structure, but with a more open landscape carrying much larger units and less hedge and tree cover than at present.

The high inputs necessary to maintain reclaimed blanket bog under adverse climatic conditions have been amply demonstrated following years of research by An Foras Taluntais at Glenamoy, Co Mayo and future reclamation is likely to be limited to the occasional expansion of existing holdings or improvement of rough grazing. Even then, without a high level of management, the reclaimed area may quickly revert to a modified form of the original peatland vegetation. Rough grazing, especially on the extensive commonages in the west and on mountains, is likely to continue, with low landscape impact except where excessive stocking density contributes to peatland erosion.

Forestry

Although just over half of our state forests are on peatland, only a small proportion, 21,000 ha or some 6%, have been planted to date on cutover raised bogs (O'Carroll, 1984). Coniferous forestry must be regarded as a realistic option for future industrial and private cutover peatlands in the Midlands. The over-riding consideration is how one can impose a tall, uniform monoculture into a essentially flat landscape without totally swamping all vistas.

The most integrated and aesthetic forestry plantations in the Midlands today are those in the former large estates and demesnes, which now contain mixed coniferous and deciduous forests or blocks of conifers shrouded by broadleaved species. A similar approach with integrated mixed planting, especially on the plant.tion edges, and with sufficient clear areas to create an impression of only semi-enclosure, could be adopted in the flat landscape of the raised bogs. In other words a multifunctional approach to forestry, with attractive settings for leisure-based activities, increased habitat diversity, supporting a wider range of flora and fauna and, of course, timber production.

State forestry policy has until now, through the mechanism of limiting maximum acquisition price, precluded afforestation of traditionally agricultural land. This policy, coupled with developments in forest drainage and increasing knowledge of tree nutrition, has resulted in 42% of the total state forest being planted on Atlantic and Montane blanket bog. These peatlands contain areas which are visually and ecologically unique in Western Europe, they are the closest we have to "Wilderness Territory" and are of immense importance to our tourist industry. While forestry may be said to add diversity to an open landscape, it is frequently implemented in a very unifunctional, unsympathetic fashion, with straight "acquisition-line" edges or total planting which completely obscures the subtleties and nuances of the blanket bog landscape.

In their study "Irish Bogs - A Case for Planning" research students from the Catholic University, Nijmegen, in the Netherlands, analysed conflicts likely to arise between utilisation options and ecological, scientific and landscape interests, and concluded that in the case of blanket bogs, afforestation was by far the land use option in greatest conflict with landscape interests (van Eck, 1984). However, not all afforestation need be detrimental and again a more broadly-based, multifunctional approach, with judicious selection of species and plantation layout, could frequently complement this unique terrain.

Preservation

A list of peatland sites worthy of preservation has been compiled by the wildlife section of the Forest & Wildlife Service. Selection criteria are ecologically orientated, but many of the areas also contain or comprise excellent examples of the various peatland landscapes. Out of a total recommended area of 43,000 ha, only 5,600 ha, or 13%, have been protected to date, through acquisition or within designated National Parks - see Table 1.

The most important question is how can a small country with a current budget deficit and an enormous foreign debt afford to preserve pristine examples of it's peatland landscape and exercise control over the development or reintegration of other peatland areas. The answer, obviously, does not lie in the outright public acquisition of all areas, but may exist in the realm of management agreements, with an appropriate range of incentives and controls.

Considerable sums of money are currently utilised to support the production of agricultural produce already in surplus within the European Economic Community. The redirection of a small proportion of this budget would allow the development and implementation of management and production (or compensation) agreements less detrimental to the peatland landscape.

While continued expansion of our forest estate may be economically and strategically desirable, the State Forest Service should reappraise its policy in relation to peatland areas, with a further broadening of its production-orientated approach, ensuring a higher level of design or amenity input to plantations in outstanding landscape areas. Similar inputs could apply in the case of private forests operating under the grants system in these areas.

In relation to private peat fuel production, no provision exists under the 1981 Turf Development Act to preclude a private developer from receiving grant aid to produce peat in an area of exceptionally high landscape quality.

The creation of a Peatlands Resource Committee, representing all of the sectoral interests - including fuel production, forestry, agriculture, landscape, game, scientific and ecological interests - has been proposed (van Eck, 1984). This committee would identify and co-ordinate the currently diverse approaches to peatland utilisation, and attempt to produce an integrated resource management strategy for Irish peatlands. Failure to go at least part of the way along this road, and to redirect some of our current policies, will undoubtedly result in the continued erosion and depletion of our future peatland landscapes.

References

Barry, T.A. (1969). Origins and Distribution of Peat Types in the Bogs of Ireland. Irish Forestry 26 (2).

Carey, M.L. and Hammond, R.F. (1970) The Soils Beneath the Midland Peats. Irish Forestry 27 (1) 23-36

Drennan, M.J., Cole, A.J., O'Dwyer, J. and McNally, G. (1984) Beef Production from Grass Grown on Peatland. Proc. 7th Int. Peat Congress, Dublin. Vol. III 264-274

Hammond, R.F. (1979) The Peatlands of Ireland. Soil Survey Bulletin No. 35, An Foras Taluntais, Dublin 58pp.

Healy, J. (1980) Industrial Cutaway Bog Development in Ireland.
Proc. 6th Int. Peat Congress, Duluth. 387-397

MacNaeidhe, F.S. et al. (1981) An Investigation of Cereal Production
on Bord na Mona Milled-Over Peatland.
Unpublished An Foras Taluntais Report.

O'Carroll, N. (1984) Peatland Afforestation in the Republic of
Ireland.
Procs. 7th Int. Peat Congress, Dublin, Vol III, 450-461

Ryan, J.B. and Cross, J.R. (1984) The Conservation of Peatlands
in Ireland.
Procs. 7th Int. Peat Congress, Dublin, Vol I, 388-406.

van Eck, H. et al (1984) Irish Bogs - A Case for Planning.
Planologisch Instituut, Katholieke Universiteit, Nijmegen,
The Netherlands, 333pp.

RURAL LANDSCAPE AND THE PLANNER

J.M. Shine

Landscape is the result of natural processes and human activities.
While man can to an extent shape the landscape, the landscape is an
important part of his physical and psychological environment and a
pervasive influence on his activities. The landscape serves as a
reference frame and a source of experience; even if, as has been
said, man is the measure of all things, he must nevertheless for his
psychological well-being establish and orientate himself securely in
space and time, and the visual elements of the landscape are a vital
basis for this. A vast output of pictorial art of varying quality
certifies to the range of emotions which landscape can induce, from
fear, through loneliness to melancholy, nostalgia, familiarity,
comfort and warmth. It must follow that variety in landscape produces a more stimulating psychological environment. Moreover, it
would seem no more than logical that, when human activities begin to
have a significant impact on the landscape, we should try to assess
whether the cumulative result is enrichment or an impoverishment of
man's environment. While the modern notion of landscape as a resource
(e.g. for the tourism industry) is one easily grasped by most people,
the older idea of landscape as a cultural resource, of indigenous
man at one with and stimulated by his visual environment, is not so
easily understood. Our very familiarity with the landscape can breed
complacency about it and limit our awareness of its cultural and
psychological importance. For the same reasons, erosion of environmental quality may not become perceptible to most people until it is

well advanced. One of the functions of the practitioner in rural planning must be to monitor landscape changes, to be a Cassandra and anticipate future disasters and try to avert them. It is also his function to seek out opportunities for beneficial change.

Clearly there are two broad sets of circumstances in which this can be accomplished, either by direct action by some agency of such all-embracing power as to be able to modify the various components of the landscape or by some agency which can control the actions of others as they affect landscape. In other words, modification can be by positive action or by passive control. These approaches to landscape modification are not mutually exclusive, but whether either of them or any combination of them is usable depends on the extent to which the constitutional rights of private property are circumscribed.

The legislative framework for the limitation of private property rights in Ireland is comprised of the various Local Government (Planning and Development) Acts, most notably the primary act of 1963. It is worth quoting the full title of the 1963 Act. "An Act to make provision, in the interests of the common good, for the proper planning and development of cities, towns, other areas (whether urban or rural including the preservation and improvement of the amenities thereof), to make certain provisions with respect to acquisition of land, to repeal the town and regional Planning Acts, 1934 & 1939 and certain other enactments and to make provision for other matters connected with the matters aforesaid".

Thus the Act in its title and certain of its sections clearly circumscribes the untrammelled use of private property by the notion

of the common good and sets up the Local Authority as arbiter of
what that common good is. However, that is not to say that the
Local Authority itself has unlimited freedom and the Act is very
careful to place a duty on it to say as clearly as possible, and in
an objective and coherent way removed from the pressure of decisions
on individual development, what the policies and objectives are
which combine to define its vision of the common good.

While, other than in the title, the word rural is not used in
the 1963 Act, it is clearly included in the "other" areas referred
to in Section 19 of the 1963 Act which <u>requires</u> the Planning Authority
to state objectives for "development and renewal of obsolete areas"
and for "preserving, improving and extending amenities". One must
delve further into the Act to see if this can be construed as con-
ferring on the Local Authority the power to plan or influence
developments which may modify the rural landscape. The Third
Schedule of the Act specifies objectives which may be included in
the Development Plan, and those which may be helpful in giving sharper
definitions to the role of the Planning Authority in relation to
rural landscape are as follows:-

THIRD SCHEDULE

"8. Providing for works incidental to the making, improvement or
landscaping of any road, including the erection of bridges, tunnels
and subways and shelters, the provision of artificial lighting and
seats and the planting or protecting of grass, trees and shrubs on
or adjoining such road.

PART II

Structures

3. Reserving or allocating any particular land, or all land in any particular area, for structures of a specified class or classes, or prohibiting or restricting either permanently or temporarily the erection, construction or making of any particular class or classes of structures on any specified land.

4. Limiting the number of structures or the number of structures of a specified class which may be constructed, erected or made, on, or in or under any area.

5. The removal or alteration of structures which are inconsistent with the development plan.

6. Regulating and controlling -

    (b) the manner in which any land is to be laid out for the purpose of development, including requirements as to road layout, landscaping, planting;

PART IV

Amenities

1. Reserving of lands as -

    (a) open spaces, whether public or private (other than open spaces reserved under Part II of this Schedule or under the next paragraph),

4. Reserving of lands for game and bird sanctuaries.

5. Preservation of buildings of artistic, architectural or historical interest.

6. Preservation of caves, sites, features and other objects of archaeological, geological or historical interest.

7. Preservation of views and prospects and of amenities of places and features of natural beauty or interest.

8. (a) Preservation and protection of woods.

   (b) Preservation and protection of trees, shrubs, plants and flowers.

9. Prohibiting, restricting or controlling, either generally or in particular places or within a specified distance of the centre line of all roads or any specified road, the erection of all or any particular forms of advertisement structure or the exhibition of all or any particular forms of advertisement.

10. Preventing, remedying or removing injury to amenities arising from the ruinous or neglected condition of any structure, or from the objectionable or neglected condition of any land attached to a structure or abutting on a public road or situate in a residential area.

11. Prohibiting, regulating or controlling the deposit or disposal of waste materials and refuse, the disposal of sewage and the pollution of rivers, lakes, ponds, gullies and the seashore.

13. Preservation of any existing public right of way giving access to seashore, mountain, lakeshore, riverbank, or other place of natural beauty or recreational utility."

Thus it can be seen that a Planning Authority has clear enough guidelines as to how it may define its role in relation to landscape conservation and improvement and it must be said that the parameters given are generous in their intent.

However, the general principle enshrined in the constitution that curtailment of an individual property right in the common interest should be the subject of reasonable compensation must be addressed and the Act goes to considerable lengths to define the circumstances in which compensation is <u>not</u> payable. In the present context, it is of interest to note that the refusal of Permission to develop based on the necessity of preserving any view or prospect of special amenity value or special interest does not incur any danger of the Planning Authority having to pay compensation. Further, conditions attached to a Permission to develop which control the size, height, character, design, colour and materials of structures, reserving land for a particular purpose, or prohibiting or restricting the erection of any particular class of structures on any land, or imposition of requirements as to the landscaping and planting do not incur any liability to compensation.

Yet again, Part V of the 1963 Act contains 11 sections empowering Planning Authorities to establish areas of special amenity if they are of outstanding natural beauty, have special recreational value, or if there is a need for nature conservation (the effect of the Special Amenity Area Order would be to establish more stringent control on development); to open up views and prospects; to preserve trees, groups of trees and woodlands; to protect from killing, taking or destruction any flora or fauna of special amenity value or special interest. As an aside here, it must be stated that there are many ways of "skinning a polecat" and, as with the conservation of buildings, malevolent neglect or other perfectly legal acts can as surely destroy flora and fauna as such action can manoeuvre a Planning Authority into an impossible situation.

If the practitioner in rural and landscape planning were to delve no deeper he might retain the comfortable feeling that he had at least a pretty solid legislative framework within which to operate, but delve deeper he must into the mire of "exemptions".

First, Government Departments are exempted from control by the Planning Authority as a matter of general legal principle. Secondly, works referred to in the Land Reclamation Act, 1949 are exempted under Section 4 of the Planning Act, that is to say:-

> (a) field drainage, (b) land reclamation, (c) the construction and improvement of watercourses, (d) the removal of unnecessary fences, (e) the construction of new fences, and the improvement of existing ones, (f) the improvement of hill grazing, and (g) the reclamation of estuarine marsh land and of callows.

Further, unless the area has been formally defined as one of special amenity, the regulations exempt the erection of structures related to mining (placed on land for less than 12 months), the erection of large agricultural buildings and yards for intensive livestock rearing, and the erection of other agricultural buildings of unlimited size from any control other than some minor restrictions as to their distance from a public road.

In short, the activities of the Department of Defence, Department of Fisheries and Forestry, the Office of Public Works (Arterial Drainage Section) and those who own and control most of the rural land, the farmers, are wholly or mostly outside the control of the planner and this severely curtails the amount of

practical control he can exercise. To be absolutely fair, he
could not, in any event, concentrate entirely on the objective
of protecting landscape regardless of the genuine needs of
development, but nevertheless, if the planner is expected to take
a balanced view of the sometimes conflicting needs of different
types of development and further the general needs of conservation,
he may sometimes feel it a bit less than logical that he is not
trusted fully to take a balanced view of rural landscape planning.

It is the general experience that members of the farming
community, by and large, feel that they should not be subjected
to such control which is seen as inimical to the efficient running
of their affairs. This is a matter which should be debated much
more, because it does not seem to many reasonable people outside
the farming business that it is any more logical to exempt modern
farming from the financial, economical and physical framework than
any other form of development.

As to the government departments, it must be said of them that
the evidence exists that they are conscious of the necessity of
consulting with planning authorities but are frequently constrained
by legislation which limits them to taking a narrow view of their
role. Thus the Office of Public Works must concentrate on drainage
i.e. lowering watertables, and the Department of Fisheries,
Forestry & Wildlife may not prohibit the felling of trees solely
for amenity reasons.

Having satisfied himself as to the legal framework within
which he must operate, the planner can then set about establishing
what exactly the policies for landscape protection and enhancement

should be. His first concern is to beware of platitudes. Landscape conservation, like morality, is popular with everyone, while it is discussed in general terms; it is only when one gets down to particulars that the differences begin to arise and one can be certain that, as with someone resisting the moralist, the despoiler of landscape will not admit to being a sinner but will simply deny the capacity and judgement of his accuser. It is therefore wise to build one's landscape "morals" on some sort of analysis that will stand up to objective scrutiny.

There are well-established approaches to landscape analysis which seem so obvious as to be hardly worth enumerating but, if only to emphasise the necessity of a systematic approach, some basic aspects of analysis are now referred to.

First, landscape is the visible expression of the structure of an area. It will have evolved from a set of events maybe millions of years ago which established the basic land forms. Secondly, these basic land forms, while in themselves unlikely to be susceptible to major modification by man, can have added to them surface effects which may substantially alter our perception of them. Thirdly, landscape is most often perceived from a moving rather than a static viewpoint - one moves through landscape much more often and for longer periods than one stands still in it.

It is therefore necessary to have a scale of qualities as well as a method of description by type and by character. An Foras Forbartha (1977) has produced a useful system of analysis in which it suggests that four categories of quality should be used:-

Sublime: Vast sweeping landscape of highest scenic quality.
           This is shown by dramatic scenery with extreme values
           of grandeur, scale, contrast and irregularity, where
           obvious signs of man's activity are at a minimum.

Highly Scenic: Of very high quality but falling short of the
           sublime category.

Scenic: Clearly more attractive than ordinary countryside,
           probably having some specific features of interest.

Rural: Ordinary countryside where no outstanding feature
           distinguishes it.

Scenery of the sublime category is likely to be open mountain
and upland, or coastal cliff area, which are exposed, and with
broad expansive views, while at the other - rural end of the
spectrum the scale is likely to be small with relatively closed
views and many significant features are likely to be man-made, such
as hedgerows, groups of trees, clearings etc. Particularly in
relation to lowland areas, it is also worth distinguishing a
variety which might best be described as 'beautiful', where there
is a particular balance and mellowness brought about by the disposition of the landscape components. This is frequently the type
of landscape most susceptible to producing good photographs - where
the composition is "pictorial". These beautiful landscapes could
perhaps be included in the broad category of the sublime. Another
category of landscape, likely to be small in scale, is the special-
interest category where a peculiarity of geomorphology or even land
use may make it striking.

In analysing an area for landscape character and quality it should be broken up into areal units which are self-contained. This is more easily done when the terrain has strong features and generally the eye will fairly easily establish a "boundary line". Thus in the National Coastline Study (1973) it was possible by visual means to establish that strip of land of considerable variation in width which "read" as being visually part of the coastline. Horizons, where significant changes of ground level occur, will define the areas. The analysis should be by the use of maps, defining visual tracts and major and minor views within them.

The direction, angle, and extent of these views should be noted. Extent can be defined as closed - where it is mainly the foreground i.e. up to half a mile; limited - open to the middle distance or a few miles; open - where the background in the distance is visible. It is usual to consider mainly views from roads in this analysis but if there is any likelihood of valuable views being available from other locations, such that they may be them-selves   established as "destinations", they should also be included.

The character of the landscape is then considered under the following headings:-

    (a) Landform

        (i)   Relief   - high, medium or low.

       (ii)   Topography   - flat, sloping, undulating land, valley.

(iii) Features   - crags and cliffs, outcrops, screes, peaks, hills etc.

(b) Ground Cover

    (i) Moorland   - heather, bracken, grass or mixed moorland, bog, scattered trees.

    (ii) Woodland   - broadleaved, coniferous or mixed, with an indication of commercial or amenity management.

    (iii) Scrub and rough grazing

    (iv) Farmland   - pasture, arable or mixed, well kept hedges and walls etc.

(c) Water

    (i) Lakes   - extent, islands, shore type.

    (ii) Rivers   - size, form i.e. shallow mountain stream or wide lowland river, meanders etc.

(d) Coastal

    (i) Relief   - high, medium or low.

    (ii) Features   - strands, beaches , rocks, cliffs, dunes.

(e) Scale

    (i) Open   - moorland, strand

    (ii) Enclosed   - field pattern, size of fields, presence of stone walls, hedges, trees and copses, shelterbelts etc.

(f) Focal Points

Churches, mansions, follies, farms and cottages etc.

(g) Detractors

Unsightly conspicuous or derelict buildings, badly sited
agricultural buildings, tips, power lines, cement works,
caravan sites, wire fences, straight edges to plantations
on hillsides, litter etc.

(h) Elements Undergoing Change.

(i) Settlements

(j) Major Views.

If this analysis is sufficiently detailed it should simplify
consideration of how any proposed development will affect the landscape and will also suggest action which might be taken to enhance
the landscape.

The surveyor will be left with a basis on which to set priorities for landscape conservation, enhancement and exploitation and it
should provide a framework within which to consider the effect on
the landscape of particular developments. It is to be hoped that
the difference in effect between siting a development on open
exposed moorland, or on a bare cliff top and tucking it into a fold
in the ground which has heavy vegetation cover will be obvious to
any developer, but between these extremes are many gradations of
effect which will vary as the characteristics of the landscape vary
and to which the response of the development controller can vary.

This form of analysis can therefore be used to draw up a hier-
archy of areas or zones in which landscape protection and/or
enhancement will have greater or lesser importance in the general

appraisal of any proposal for development.

At this point it is important to stress again that land-scape is one of a number of factors to be weighed in ascertaining whether a particular development is on balance positive or negative in physical planning terms.

It is usual in Statutory Development Plans to indicate areas of high amenity and views and prospects which it is an objective to protect, but the provisions are generally stated broadly leaving the way open for more detailed analysis of the type referred to above to be used as a tool to help in decision making on individual development proposals. The criticism is sometimes made that Statutory Development Plans are too vague on landscape matters to be useful in clarifying for potential developers in rural areas what will or will not be acceptable, and to an extent this critic-ism may be justified. There are areas where analysis of the kind referred to will indicate quite clearly that almost any development would have such an adverse effect that it is quite unacceptable and if this is so it should be stated unequivocally. It is a very important function of the planner to articulate clearly the reasons for any policy so as to gain public acceptance, and land-scape policy is no exception to this rule. In articulating land-scape policy it is important to stress the role of the landscape as a resource both for direct exploitation as an attraction for the tourism business and as a culture resource for the citizens at large. There are two difficulties that must be faced in this line of argument; first, the best scenery is not unusually sited where the inhabitants are poorest and, secondly, the simplest and most

immediate way in which they can exploit the resource is by selling
off pieces of it. However, arguments based on these premises have
to be considered as being on a par with those which claim that wind-
fall profits gained by landowners on the edges of developing towns,
and arising out of the fortuitous proximity of services paid for by
the common purse, should accrue to them alone.

Much of the rural planner's work will not involve such stark
choices as total rejection of development proposals and it is
frequently the case that he or she will be involved in trying to
secure modifications in proposals for development so as to avoid or
ameliorate adverse effects on the landscape and possibly to use
the opportunity for some landscape enhancement. It is, at first
analysis, a surprising fact that in a country that is urbanising
fairly rapidly the largest part of a rural planner's work in development control relates to the building of individual houses. As an
aside it might be said here that the greatest failure of twenty
years of physical planning in Ireland is the failure to produce a
more acceptable form of town and village design or indeed to
provide an adequate framework within which people can own the kind
of house they aspire to within an urban or village area. This
large section of the housing market has been left to the vagaries
of "market forces" resulting in a pioneer population of urban folk
searching the countryside for sites. As one landowner or another
receives a letter from his Bank Manager, gets tired of farming,
wants to send his daughter to College, the bête noir of the rural
planner, the "urban-generated rural house" emerges in as random a
pattern as space invaders in a video game. Because of the fact

referred to previously that landscape is experienced by moving
through it, not only the individual effect but also the cumulative
effect of a number of such houses must be considered. The curtilage
of the new residences is generally no larger than it must be, the
building-line close to the road, the opportunities for screening
minimal, and it takes little enough of such development to create
an extensive pocket of landscape which is neither urban nor rural,
(and despite the aspirations of all of the individuals involved
does not add up to a coherent alternative). The hedgerows of the
real countryside are breached intermittently by stretches of
plastered walls, wrought iron gates and tarmacadam driveways.
Roadside drainage is disrupted, cable servicing follows the line
of the roads and the conflict between it and the existing or
potential roadside trees is immediately apparent. Apart altogether
from the other planning problems involved the landscape problems
leave everyone, including the individual developers, vaguely
dissatisfied and nobody quite knows what to do. One suggestion
has been to concentrate such development into small pockets of
houses, but given the market forces by which the housing is created
and the normal pattern of landholdings it can readily be seen that
this is not practicable. A green-belt policy is almost the only
workable one; the urban or village areas would be clearly defined
and outside of them only housing needs directly related to farming
would be catered for. This may in turn transfer some of the problem
further out into the rural area, but lack of enthusiasm for real
isolation, together with the fact that a larger area is available
to absorb the housing, means that in landscape terms the development

is more capable of being absorbed, at least if the surrounding
landscape falls within the broad category of 'Rural' (as earlier
defined by An Foras Forbartha). The problem then becomes one of
detail.

An unobtrusive site should be picked, where the building
avoids cutting skyline or waterline and where the minimum disruption of the existing field and hedgerow pattern is caused. Using
a corner of a field rather than carving a piece out of the middle
makes landscape as well as farming sense, providing in many cases
an extra, readymade screen. The size and configuration of the
site should be such as to avoid the likelihood of the occupants
developing a phobia about trees falling on the house. Moreover,
the architectural character of the building should at least
acknowledge that indigenous to the area. Terra-cotta tiles and
windows set back beneath the shade of arched verandas, which looked
so attractive in that little place one saw in Spain, will not
necessarily sit comfortably in the green of Ballymagash. When seen
against a rural background the red bricks available from modern
brickworks, whether placed in the house or boundary walls, will do
little to soothe the tired eye. Generally, simple styles with
horizontal emphasis to the main structure, and following broadly
the contour of the ground, will fit in best. Front boundary walls
and gate piers constructed in the style and of the materials indigenous to the area will help to integrate the development into the
landscape. In many cases the planting of native forest trees along
the rear of the site can help to tie in the mass of the building
to the landscape. Where timber is used on the site for fences, gates

etc. a dark matt finish such as that produced by creosoting will look more restful than light colours or white. It is not unreasonable to try to get cable servicing to follow unobtrusive routes and it is frequently justifiable to have it brought underground from the last pole to the house. Generally, building lines should be such as to avoid the appearance of the house being tied visually to the road. Generally a minimum building line of about 20 metres will be needed to achieve this and if less is available consideration should be given to maintaining existing hedgerows along the frontage to screen the house visually from the road.

While much farm development is exempted, nevertheless many large buildings outside the exempted development class are constructed in the rural areas and their landscape implications should be seriously considered. Often, they are planned as an extension of development on a site where existing farm buildings already form a substantial mass and this in itself can be helpful in avoiding any great disruption of landscape amenity. It is also frequently the case that trees have grown up around the site which help further to screen the buildings. The existence of such trees should be carefully noted in assessing development proposals, as should their age and condition, and the developer's intentions as to their future. There is no reason why additional planting should not be required to help to maintain the status quo in landscape terms. The nature of the materials used in such modern farm buildings gives little scope to the designer but at least where galvanised metal is used stipulations can be made as to the colour to be used when painting the building, which will not be until the galvanising has weathered.

Dark matt green is about the most satisfactory colour to use.

Less frequently, virgin sites are developed for new agricultural buildings and, if the development requires permission, the
location should be carefully considered. Here the ACOT adviser
could be of assistance at the very early stages of planning, when
the site is being chosen. While once the conventional wisdom was
that an elevated site from which rainwater and effluent could drain
away readily was best, nowadays, with the insistence on proper and
adequate effluent storage and the likelihood of effluent spills to
waterways attracting penalties, there is much to be said for choosing
a site with different characteristics and which might take landscape
considerations into account. However, it is likely that the use of
tree planting to help tie the buildings into the landscape will still
be a major factor to be considered. The siting of power lines to
such a development will also need to be handled as sensitively as
possible.

On the question of farm development, farm buildings, and the
use of trees to enhance or preserve landscape amenity there is a
point worth considering, not only by the planner but by the ACOT
adviser and the Department of Agriculture's grant inspector.
Frequently, farm development work which is exempted development is
first carried out e.g. the removal of fences, hedgerows etc. resulting in the formation of what might euphemistically be called much
more open landscape. Shortly afterwards an application for permission
is made in respect of buildings which require it. If the removal of
trees which had taken place previously were to be regarded as part
of the development, it would be permissible for the planner to

require the planting of trees as compensation for those removed. This could be done by planting copses in corners which are not readily accessible by modern farming machinery and would in time produce an interesting if more open landscape. A further point should be made in relation to trees on the farm landscape. There appears to be a clear difference of opinion between silviculturists and agriculturists as to the value of shelter belts. There can be no doubt where the planner's sympathies would lie from the point of view of landscape amenity.

The planner does, of course, have a major weapon in his armoury in relation to trees in the landscape, in the Tree Preservation Order. Indeed so powerful a weapon does it appear to be that many planning authorities tend to view it as the U.S. & U.S.S.R. view the atomic bomb - never to be used lest retaliation be swift and painful. (In the form of a compensation claim!) The truth is, of course, more prosaic and helpful. The making of a Tree Preservation Order brings the matter of cutting trees or woodland within the ambit of the permission regulations made under Section 24 of the 1963 Planning Act - nothing more. If an order is made in respect of a tree or a group of trees which the planning authority declares to be of special amenity value it may refuse to grant permission for their removal without any fear of attracting a successful compensation claim. It can grant permission for the felling of woodland which will require its replanting, and it can have the felling done in such a way as to ensure continuity of the woodland, rather than clear felling. In this, the author's experience is that the fullest co-operation of the Department of Fisheries & Forestry is assured.

Thus, much can be done to protect existing trees and woodland which are of value in the landscape, but there is the practical problem of establishing priorities to be taken into account. In practical terms the planner will frequently find that the trees to which a Tree Preservation Order has been attached are not under threat while ones which he didn't get around to examining are the subject of an application for a felling licence, or, worse, already under attack without reference to anyone. It must be borne in mind that trees which are diseased and dangerous cannot be made the subject of a Tree Preservation Order. However, the question of what degree of danger it represents needs much more attention. It is difficult to accept that some of the trees that have been removed in the name of safety were in fact a threat to anyone and much more use should be made of qualified silviculturists to ascertain if some solution other than complete removal might not be applied.

Reference to trees in the landscape must include the activities of the Department of Fisheries and Forestry. Indeed it is arguable that their activities have to-date had a more significant effect on landscape than any other rural development - much of it beneficial. The rural planner is not in a position to exert any direct control over forestry development, but generally co-operation exists between the department and the planning authorities which would enable the planner to have some influence on the landscape effect of afforestation. This is an area which has been insufficiently explored. The forester's main brief is to plant trees for commercial exploitation and this must place certain restrictions on him, but it should nevertheless be possible to consider the landscape implications of afforestation of particular places. Even simple things like varying the planting distance from a road or stream and using mixed plantings of native species along margins can have a visual effect whose amenity value far outweighs any loss of production. The planting of a relatively small number of specimen trees in a stand to be left intact during clear felling can help to retain a sense of woodland. Where roadside fences of sod and stone exist, sheep-proof fencing might be planted behind the fence rather than on top of it. These things are well within the competence of the rural planner and local forestry inspector to agree between them.

Other landscape considerations in relation to forestry which would justify wider-ranging analysis are the effects of large-scale planting on the visual quality of the basic topography of an area. Large areas of monoculture can easily produce an amorphous blanket over an area which blots out rock outcrops, streams, drainage gulleys and other topographic features which all add variety and visual interest. Such landscapes could be analysed with a view to a planting regime which would emphasise some of the topographical features and might suggest areas or features which could be left "undeveloped". The longer-term implications of the development of forest roads for maintenance and final cropping could also be considered. It does not seem unreasonable that the Forest and Wildlife Services should undertake such an analysis. Even if something as vague as the common good did not appear sufficient justification it could be borne in mind that treating forest landscape as a tourist resource could bring a direct financial return.

Activities of the local authority itself, such as road construction

and realignment, water impoundment and refuse disposal, can have
very significant landscape effects and the rural planner must have
an input into their design and on occasions their location. In
these developments, with the possible exception of dumps, design
considerations other than landscape will of necessity be the dominant ones but it is almost always the case that roads can benefit
readily from landscaping and can present new opportunities to open
up views and prospects. The planning authority may also prohibit
the erection of advertising hoardings in rural areas, while water
impoundments will provide many improvements in landscape quality if
handled with sensitivity. Dumps are such an emotive issue that it
may be impossible to find a location which does not produce a very
strong reaction. Possibly the solution is to acquire land by
stealth a generation ahead of its likely use and exercise every
possible opportunity to sterilise the surrounding area for other
development, meanwhile planting massive screening at least a half
mile in depth around the area in the hope that by the time its use
is required there will be nobody around to object!

Quarrying operations for stone or gravel tend generally to be
fairly compact in the areas which they affect and it is usually
possible to ameliorate their adverse visual effect by controlling
the location of plant, waste tips etc., and by requiring rehabilit-
ation of worked-out areas in phase with the development as well as
making use of screen planting. The control of dust both from the
process and from transport of material can have an important implication for landscape values in the vicinity. Lack of adequate dust
control can adversely affect the vegetation in the vicinity.

The winning of peat by mechanical means has to be carried
out in such an extensive operation that,while it is always carried
out in low-lying areas,it can have a profound effect on landscape.
The areas in which peat exploitation occurs have few enough contrasting landscape types, hence the importance of taking whatever
practical steps are possible to minimise its impact. Leaving
substantial reserves of virgin bog adjacent to roadways would seem
the best way of doing this. Careful planting of appropriate tree
species in a manner replicating the natural sequence of ecological
development could be used to give additional screening of the
sections being exploited.

Electricity and telecommunication transmissions require
development which is rarely in sympathy with the rural landscape
and the rural planner is often in considerable difficulty in dealing
with them. Decisions in principle as to routes and sites are often
taken at regional or national level before any consultation takes
place at county level, and the planner may find that a decision
taken in an adjoining county compromises his freedom of choice as to
a route or a site in his jurisdiction. In the last analysis, however,
control lies with the planning authority and lack of consultation
at the appropriate time does not entitle developers to engage in any
special pleading. Similarly, where private enterprise reception
and re-distribution of television signals is proposed, lack of consultation with the planning authority prior to applications for
licences can create subsequent situations of conflict, but it does
appear as if technological advances may dispel the spectre of every
hillock adorned with a large receiving antenna.

It should be carefully noted by all concerned that it is <u>not</u>
essential to place telephone cables along roadside fences. Care with
the siting of lines is becoming more and more important as the
number of routes increases and the appearance of lines deteriorates.

The countryside abounds in items of historic, architectural,
archaeological and scientific interest. They are testimony to man's
long-term influence on the landscape, establish his place within the
natural environment, and in the press of modern urban living preserve
him from being an alien in his own land. Inevitably in the course
of progress some heritage items must be displaced, but the planner
has a duty to call attention to their presence and to ensure at
least that they are not swept carelessly aside. Thus, planning
authorities in their development plans publish large lists of items
which must be considered for preservation if any development is
proposed which would endanger their future existence. In most
cases development can be modified to minimise the threat and landowners generally are more likely to be proud than disappointed to be
told that they are custodians of part of our national heritage. Why
then, one must ask, is so much of it disappearing? The answer must
lie in the fact that the listings are of such relatively recent
currency that there has not been time for the message to sink in,
or possibly that changes of management of landholdings occur in
such a way that new managers may not even be aware of the listings.
It is difficult to escape the impression that here again the case
for requiring all agricultural development to be the subject of an
application for permission should be considered.

Even where a new development in a rural area does not require

the actual removal of a heritage item their location vis-a-vis
each other needs to be taken into account. For its proper appreciation as an item in the landscape as well as an historical state-
ment, a heritage item may need to stand alone protected by its own
"green belt" or amenity area as it is usually described. It is to
be hoped that even the most mercenary developer will see the
offensiveness of a television mast beside Grianan Aileach or a farm
building adjacent to Poulnabrone Dolmen, but the same principle
applies to all field monuments and buildings and is reinforced in
archaeological terms by the likelihood of valuable data being
scattered around as well as inside the structure.

Reference has been made to advertising hoardings in the context of road development. Such hoardings have no place in rural
areas and should not be allowed. Smaller advertisements also need
firm control. Anything other than rigid prohibition will result in
a visually chaotic situation with the competing signs of purveyors
of goods and services playing leapfrog along the approaches to towns
and villages. A valid distinction can be made between informative
and competitive signposting. The local authorities operate a
uniform system of informative signposting and a similar system can
cater adequately for facilities which need to advertise their
presence in rural areas. In one rural county at least, a system of
fingerpost signs is used to indicate the locations of facilities
catering for travellers which are situated off the main routes.
A distinctive colour is used (in this case white lettering on a
blue background). This enables the traveller seeking such a
facility to home in on the sign from a moving vehicle at about the

same distance at which large hoardings trying to perform the same function would become effective, but the visual effect is unobtrusive. Efforts are being made to standardise this approach throughout the region. Proprietors of premises offering facilities consider the system to be effective in balancing the advantage enjoyed by facilities sited on the main routes, and the planning authority considers that it eases the pressure for the establishment of such facilities as guesthouses solely along the more heavily trafficked routes. Other facilities can be signposted by fingerposting in the ordinary way using the standard black and white fingerposting but consideration could be given to a more elaborate colour coding. A further facility which is about to be put into operation is the provision, at laybys, of area maps, set horizontally and orientated correctly which would have a surround in which could be inserted small advertisements related particularly to tourist business and facilities in the area covered by the map. It is considered that these approaches will provide a better advertisement for the tourist industry than the alternative of unsightly proliferations of hoardings.

While landscape is not the only consideration on which the rural planner must concentrate it is clearly a major aspect of his work and must, to varying degrees, be a factor in almost all development control work. Equally, landscape enhancement and exploitation must form a large part of that section of his brief which is concerned with innovation and initiative. The help which he can expect from bodies such as An Foras Forbartha, and to a widely varying extent An Taisce, is very valuable. An Foras, through its research and publications on specifically Irish topics related to rural planning, landscape and amenity and its Conservation and Amenity Advisory Scheme, has made a contribution which the writer is very happy to acknowledge. Consideration should be given by government departments such as Fisheries & Forestry, Agriculture, the Department of Finance (Office of Public Works), and Semi-State Organisations such as Bord Failte, Bord na Mona, and E.S.B. to the more widespread and continuous use of an expanded landscape advisory service. The National Coastline Study (1973) which An Foras Forbartha and Bord Failte sponsored was an invaluable guide to maritime planning authorities. Similar studies for other areas of the country might be undertaken, as might the necessary studies for Special Amenity Area Orders. The necessity for continuing education for rural planners is obvious and the setting up of the Rural Planners Forum within the Irish Planning Institute is welcome, as is the joint approach of An Foras, the Irish Planning Institute, the Royal Town Planning Institute, and University College, Dublin to the provision of Continuing Education Seminars.

Landscape enhancement will not occur in a financial vacuum and somewhere a replacement for the "improving landlords" of earlier days must be found. It may be that the Social Employment Schemes now being mooted, if organised in a more flexible and generous way as to expenditure on materials, will enable local authorities to adopt a bigger role in positive schemes of landscape improvement, but it is important, if this is to happen, that the scale of development funds be significant. A series of pilot projects involving the combined efforts of local and state bodies with an input from An Foras Forbartha and Bord Failte suggests itself. Such projects

could even form part of a larger scheme of development of the
tourism industry in particular locations, involving the development
and marketing of accommodation and activities and the revival of
traditional rural industries, all of which would in turn create a
greater awareness of landscape as a basic renewable resource.

References

An Foras Forbartha, Inventory of Outstanding Landscapes in Ireland,
Dublin, 1977.

    do.   Planning for Amenity, Recreation & Tourism,
Dublin, 1970.

    do.   County Lists of Sites of Historic/Artistic
Importance.

Bord Failte Eireann/An Foras Forbartha, National Coastline Study,
Dublin, 1973.

Crowe, Silvia, The Landscape of Forests & Woods, Forestry
Commission, London, 1978.

The Environmental Council, A Policy for the Environment, Dublin,
1980.

Fairbrother, N., New Lives, New Landscapes, London, 1970.

Institute of Landscape Architects, Landscape & Tourist Development
Conference Proceedings, Cork, 1970.